If you have the courage to face what millions of children face each day, then read this book. Catalin's *Odyssey* will tear into your heart as you experience a child's life on the streets. This is not a story you can ignore, because there are children like Catalin living in every city in every nation of the world. And if you haven't seen them living in the garbage dumps, the dark alley ways or the steaming sewers of *your* city, maybe it's time you did. After reading this book, you won't be able to walk away. It's time you walked down Catalin's street.

—Bill Wilson
Founder and Pastor
Metro Ministries
Brooklyn, New York

Odyssey of a Romanian Street Child

Cătălin Dobrişan and John Kachelmyer

CREATION
HOUSE PRESS.

ODYSSEY OF A ROMANIAN STREET CHILD
by Catalin Dobrisan and John Kachelmyer
Published by Creation House Press
A part of Strang Communications Company
600 Rinehart Road
Lake Mary, Florida 32746
www.creationhouse.com

Cover design by Judy McKittrick
Interior design by David Bilby

Library of Congress Catalog Card Number: 2002112439

International Standard Book Number: 0-88419-941-X

02 03 04 05 87654321
Printed in the United States of America

CONTENTS

IMPORTANT INFORMATION

Catalin: Pronounced *Kuh-tuh-leen*, with the accent on the last syllable.

Gara de Nord (North Station): Bucharest's main train station.

Aurolac: (gilding lacquer) A volatile aluminum stove paint. The fumes, when inhaled, produce a sensation akin to drunkenness.

John: An American who came in January 1993 to help street kids; called Daddy by all the children.

Bucharest: Romania's capital city.

Ceausescu: Romania's Communist dictator from 1965 to 1989.

Transylvania: An area in north-central and northwestern Romania formerly belonging to Hungary but ceded to Romania in 1918. The population remains approximately 50 percent ethnic Hungarian. There is also a large ethnic German population.

The Revolution: The overthrow of the Communist government December 22, 1989.

INTRODUCTION

The first time I met Catalin—January 5, 1995—he was fifteen years old. It was a cold, raw day. A bone-chilling wind was blowing, and slush stood ankle deep in the streets. It was early afternoon, and I had just gotten off a train at the Gara de Nord, Bucharest's main train station. A group of street kids met me, most of whom I knew. Among those I didn't know was Catalin. The first thing I noticed about him was that he was wearing a T-shirt and, otherwise, was covered only by a threadbare summer suit coat. I was bundled in a heavy winter coat and my head covered by a Russian fur hat. "How can he bear the cold?" I wondered.

I took all the boys who met me to an inexpensive restaurant where the owner didn't mind their shabby clothing and dirt-encrusted hands and faces as long as I paid the bill. Afterwards, Catalin insisted on showing me where he "lived." We stomped through the slush, and as we passed a flower shop, one of the boys asked for money to buy candles. The flower shop sold them for wakes. I was soon to find out what the boys wanted them for. We entered the Gara, and I was guided to an unobtrusive door that opened off an exit from the station. Behind the door was a landing with stairways going up and down. I was led down into a subterranean passageway and Stygian darkness. Suddenly I knew why we had bought the candles. Windowless rooms opened off a long corridor, and at the end, stood one room larger than the others. The boys seemed pleased I had come and announced that this was their home, as proud as if it were a mansion. The room was slightly warmer than the corridor because a steam pipe ran through it.

The first thing I noticed was that the floor was almost knee deep in crumpled paper. The room had been used to store station archives, and the children tore the binders to pieces and crumpled the paper for bedding. The second thing I noticed was how close the candles were to the paper. *How is it they have not yet set the place on fire and burned up with it?* I wondered. Then I noticed that many children were already there, sitting in total darkness, when we arrived.

It wasn't until January 18, however, that I brought Catalin home along with four other boys. Even though we held first-class tickets, we had to wait in the second-class waiting room because the boys weren't allowed into the first-class waiting room, tickets or no tickets. There was only one seat available, so the boys insisted I take it; they sat on the floor around a pillar. An elderly peasant woman kept eyeing the five boys and me. Finally her curiosity could not be contained, and she asked what was going on. Someone told her that all of them were street kids and that I was taking them to a new home in Transylvania. For a moment she looked startled. Then she started bowing over and over and making the sign of the cross as if she were in the presence of something holy. All I could think was, *Would that some others besides this uneducated peasant woman could recognize that there is something sacred about helping the homeless.* After all, Jesus said, "If you give to them, you give to Me!"

The train left near midnight for the eight-hour trip. There wasn't a lot of difference between first and second class except the price, but the first-class seats could be pulled out to make a resting place. A third of the way through our journey the heat went out in our first-class compartment. Not only did the heat go out, but it was also the coldest night of the year. The boys all huddled together for warmth. I would have appreciated their comfort, but thought better of it. It wasn't the dirt they carried on them or even the smell that hovered around them like a fog, but I did draw the line at lice. I had lost most of my hair through the years, but I still had enough to provide a respectable residence for a colony of cooties. So, I kept my distance.

A few weeks later Catalin started school. Like most of the kids I brought home, he was starved. We never scrimped on food. One of the chief joys of my life has been to see hungry kids eat. Watching them, I get a big lump in my throat that doesn't want to go away, and I remember the words of Jesus: "I was hungry, and you gave Me something to eat." It is such an exhilarating experience that I wonder why more people don't do it.

One evening we had fried chicken. Catalin announced he had made friends with a hungry dog on the way to school, so I put the leftover scraps in a paper sack and gave it to him to take with him the next morning. When he returned home the next afternoon, I asked him if the dog had enjoyed the scraps. He gave me a strange, sideways look and, without saying a word, went up to his room. I looked over at the other boys for an explanation. One of them shrugged and said matter-of-factly, "Catalin ate the scraps before he got to the dog." I believe that was the last time he indulged in his old habit from his street days of eating garbage.

Five years passed. It was December 22, 1999, the tenth anniversary of the Romanian Revolution. Catalin, now twenty, and I had just watched a historical documentary, and I began to ask him questions. He had been only ten years old in 1989, but I wondered what he remembered from those days. He began to tell me story after story, late into the night. From that evening and those true accounts of his life grew this book. I trust you will find it as fascinating to read as I did to hear.

—John Kachelmyer
Targu Mures, Romania
February 2000

CHAPTER 1

Happy Days

I have lived the few short years of my life in many disparate worlds. Perhaps to some, traveling to numerous places and tasting of diverse experiences would be an exciting prospect. To me it wasn't. Although I survived, I was nearly torn apart in the process.

My life was stable in the beginning—and only now have I managed to return to a place of stability. Eight years of my life were spent in a meat grinder. How I endured I don't know. Once caught in the machine, it was virtually impossible to extricate myself without sustaining serious injury. Many other kids—in fact, the majority—caught in the same vortex as I was did not survive; their lives now a shipwreck. Only God knows why I made it and others didn't. There was nothing better in me that would attract divine favor—only that His ways are inscrutable. Many great minds have sought the answer as to why He takes one and leaves another, so I will not attempt to explain that, because I don't think it can be answered. I will only set forth my story—what happened to me—in hopes that something in it may help others gain insight as to why a child would find it preferable living in the streets to living at home.

My maternal grandfather, Balcinoiu Ion, was born in 1900. He was of the class of boyars. In Russia the boyars were a hereditary class of aristocrats, but in Romania they were, more simply, wealthy landowners. His family was rich in cattle, pigs and sheep. Their house was the largest in the village. In time, my grandfather became the mayor. His first wife bore him six children. After she died in 1941, he married again. His second wife was my grandmother, Maria. Together they had seven children. The last two were born in 1957: a set of twins, a boy and girl. The boy was my Uncle Dumitru and the girl was my mother, Nedelea. The remaining five children died before reaching the age of twenty.

After World War II, the Communists took power in Romania. Some boyars were killed outright by the government for their land—though this did not happen at once. Others were sent to work on the visionary Danube canal project along with priests, lawyers, college professors and other intellectuals. In 1962 my grandfather had all his cattle, pigs and most of his sheep taken from him in the Communist frenzy.

My grandfather died in 1967. After his death, the children from the first marriage put my grandmother out of the house, tore down the home and all the farm buildings and divided the materials among themselves. Between the heirs and the Communists, there was nothing left.

My mother finished eighth grade in 1973. She did very well in school, thanks to her mother's persistent help. She then completed two years of high school in the city of Buzau. She considered it an honor to win third place in a gymnastic competition.

Realizing that she could not finish high school, she transferred to a professional school to study electricity. In 1978 she graduated and gained employment as an electrician.

My paternal grandfather, Dobrisan Gheorghe, was born in 1914 into a family of modest means. He fought in World War II, and I heard several times how he was shot in the leg. After the war, he returned to his birth village, where he fell in love with the daughter of boyars. Her parents were adamantly against their marriage and tried, by all means, to break up the proposed union. Finding normal marriage channels blocked, my grandparents eloped. Four children were born to their union. My father, Ion, born in 1951 was one of them.

My father's childhood was lived under the strict supervision of my grandfather, who was a mentally sharp individual but also an exacting man and a maniac for organization. For that reason, my father was raised without affection. He had no example of human warmth to follow. In 1965 at fourteen years of age, after finishing the eighth grade, my father left for Brasov, one of the largest cities in Romania. There, he attended a year of professional school for prospective railroad employees. After finishing his year of schooling, he was employed as an assistant mechanic on a diesel locomotive. He worked at that for a year. The next five years he worked in a steel rolling mill. Like all able-bodied, Romanian young men, he faced a year of compulsory military service. He knew how austere that year would be. A soldier's salary did not even cover the basics. He had the wisdom to put aside money for that time so he could pass his year in ease. At age twenty-four, he was finally inducted. Indeed, his foresight enabled him to breeze through his year in a comfort the ordinary soldier could not dream of. After completing his mandatory service, he returned to Niscov, where his family lived, and found employment as a machinist.

In 1978 my mother started working at the same factory where my father was employed, and somehow, they met. Four months after meeting, they were married in a civil ceremony. Within a year, I was born in Buzau on September 26, 1979.

The first five months of my life my parents lived with my paternal grandparents. Because of the difficulty of taking care of me and working at the same time, my parents took me to my sixty-year-old maternal grandmother and left me with her to raise for the next seven years. Since my grandfather had died several years before, it was just my grandmother and I. From time to time my mother came to visit and brought me candy and clothing.

The years I lived with my grandmother were very happy ones. Nothing disturbed me. She lived in the country where the roads were made of earth. We were surrounded by farm fields. Instead of the stale smell of the city was the verdant, soothing country smell of growing things.

Many scenes remain in my memory from those days. At the edge of the nearby rustic village was a plot of rather useless ground that was used for playing football or pasturing cows. One year it rained so much, however, that the area turned into a swamp; I remember going there to swim.

There was also a vineyard where we all used to go and gather grapes. My grandmother worked at an agricultural cooperative, and my Uncle Dumitru was a shepherd. Sometimes my grandmother would take me with her when she went to work in the fields.

On rare occasions, my grandmother took me to visit my other grandparents. The area where they lived was especially beautiful. I don't remember a lot about those visits except that my paternal grandfather was a very strict and severe man. My child's instincts told me to avoid him. My paternal grandmother was not especially warm either. I have the memory of some kind of family holiday, a wedding or baptism, and my grandfather decided that was the time to teach me table manners. Apparently I didn't learn well enough, because when I asked him for more food, he refused to give it to me.

One other scene remains vividly in my memory from when I was three years old. I had gone swimming and picked up some serious illness. By the time I got home I was really sick, and I fainted in front of the house. My grandmother, not knowing what else to do, put a candle next to me where I was lying and went for help. She was expecting me to die. Some neighbors came, took my temperature and found I had a fever of 41°C (105.8°F). They called an ambulance and, while waiting, wrapped me in wet sheets to cool me down. I stayed in the hospital a week.

Despite my close call with death, I was secure in the knowledge that my grandmother loved me and would always care for me. During those days, my life was very happy. I was free. I had no responsibilities. All I had to do was eat, play, sleep and bask in my grandmother's love and attention.

It seems strange to say, but until I was five years old, I had only met my father on one or two occasions, and those I don't really remember. During those years I was with my grandmother, my mother had become pregnant again and had had three abortions. In the time of Ceausescu abortions were illegal—and contraceptives were not available. My mother went to an old woman, an abortionist, whose methods were very crude. Each time after the abortion, my mother had to go to the hospital to get "repaired." There were many women during those times who died from those crude abortions.

By both working and saving their salaries, my parents were able to buy an apartment. Thus, in 1983 they moved into the city of Buzau. Now that they had a stable place to live, they felt they could have another child, so my brother Viorel was allowed to be born in 1984.

In 1985, when I was five, my mother decided to bring me to their apartment in the city. It was the first time I could really remember being with my father. I stayed only three weeks, after which my mother took me back to my grandmother. I remember how strict my father was and how afraid I was of him. I gathered he didn't like me either. He kept talking about how when I went to school I would have to study hard. I hadn't even started school, and already I didn't like it!

In 1986 another brother was born.

CHAPTER 2

Not Good Enough

At last the time came for me to go to school, so when I was seven, my mother brought me back to the city and enrolled me in first grade. Just before school started, my father thought he would give me a head start by teaching me the numbers. It wasn't that I was dense; it was that I had never had to concentrate before, and his powerful personality was distracting. I had no idea at that point what I was in for, either then or in the future, so I was a bit inattentive.

My father pointed to a number. What was it? I gave the wrong answer. As startling as a thunderclap, Wham! His powerful hand whacked me across the head.

Stunned, my head reeling, I was too dumbfounded to know how to react. Nothing like it had ever happened to me in my whole, short life. Little did I know the terror had only begun.

First grade was horrible. I didn't learn anything at all. I made nothing but mistakes in reading and writing. I was at the bottom of my class except in sports. I remember that I got a 3 on one of my papers, and I exchanged it with a fellow student who got a 2 because to me it didn't make any difference. (In Romania, grades are given on a scale of 1 to 10. Five and up is passing. Anything below 5 is failing.) Coupled with the failure at school was the constant nagging by my father.

When school was in session, it was my father who took charge of me—of my homework and trying to bring my grades up. Whenever I got a grade of 4 I would come home in fear, knowing that I was not going to escape getting slapped around by my father. I was dreadfully frightened of him.

By the end of the first school year it became apparent I was not going to pass. It is no different in Romania than anywhere else; parents don't want their child held back a year. As I remember, in order to get me passed to the next grade, my mother took a gift to school, a large curio in the form of a rabbit.

I don't know why, but I destroyed all my toys. My father would repair them, and I would destroy them again.* Finally my father refused to repair the broken ones or buy me any new ones, so, when I was in first grade, I found myself without toys. In the fall of 1986 I stole three hundred lei of my father's money. (At that time sixty lei equaled one U.S. dollar.) I took the money and bought the toys and candy I felt I was denied. At night I hid these things, plus the unused money, outdoors under a car.

When my father found his money missing, he asked me about it. I tried to lie but didn't succeed. He questioned me from 8:00 in the morning until 1:00 in the afternoon. He was lying on his bed and had me kneel on the floor next to him. If I did not keep my back straight, he hit me with his belt. He did this for several hours, after which time I admitted what I had done—but I didn't tell him where I hid the money. He sent me to look for it, but to my surprise, it was not under the car. I panicked, but there was nothing to be done about it except go back into the apartment without the money. My father made me kneel another couple hours. I was sweating and tired.

Somehow I managed to finish first grade, after which came a vacation of three months—the joy of all students. One time, during vacation, when both my parents were at work, I started to look through things that were stored in a wardrobe out on the balcony of the apartment. I found a stack of money: ten lei banknotes, but I took only one. Then I found a large ring of keys, which I also took. Happy at my good fortune, I skipped down the stairs and outside to go buy some cotton candy. My father sometimes gave me enough money to buy one, but I was never satisfied. So I bought five and brought them back to eat on the balcony.

Later I went out again to buy some candy at the corner, about a block away. I bought quite a bit and headed home, but when I arrived back at the apartment, I found to my dismay that I had lost the keys. When my mother arrived home from work, she found me standing out in the hallway in front of our apartment door. I told her what happened.

She sent me out at once to look for the keys, saying, "If you don't find them, don't come back!"

The hallways and stairways in Romanian apartment buildings are dark. There was always a campaign to conserve electricity. Each apartment had its own electric meter, but not for gas and water. Once a month the bill for the total amount of water consumed in the entire building was added to the total amount of gas consumed and then added to the electricity used in the hallways. That was divided by the number of occupants, and each was assessed his share. Thus a family of five would pay more than a family of three. Since there were no individual meters on the gas and water, there was no incentive to conserve, which led to waste. Why conserve if the people in the next apartment were going to be extravagant and careless? Leaky faucets were allowed to run. People lit the burners on their gas stoves in the morning to cook breakfast and let them continue burning all day. Although the dim bulbs in the stairways consumed less than a minute fraction of the total utility bill, it was there that the pressure was on to conserve. Some buildings had switches that would automatically turn off after two minutes. Heading down the stairs at night, it paid not to dawdle, or the light would go out and one would stumble the rest of the way down in the dark. What was inconsistent with conservation was that the hallways were heated by hot water pipes, but often the front door of the building would not close, wasting enormous amounts of heat.

Anyhow, I headed down the dark stairway, feeling about as dark inside. After all, I didn't really know the people I was living with. I was disconnected from them—or any of the people in the city for that matter. I had been raised free. My first seven years were spent with my grandmother free from restrictions and responsibilities. All I did was play and swim. Thus, the liberty I experienced during those first seven years entered into my system. When I was taken from that and put into the city and school, I entered another world I did not know. There were responsibilities and restrictions, and I had no control over how my time was spent. The method by which all this was imposed on me was not a method done with love but by force. The problem was compounded by the fact that I really didn't know my parents, especially my father. Here was a stranger who suddenly took over my entire life and without a shred of kindness or understanding forced me into a mold—a lifestyle that was totally foreign to me. It was like being taken to another country. As I started school, my father reviewed each piece of homework I did; there wasn't a single day in which I didn't get a beating. My face was always red and swollen. I should have been embarrassed before my friends and classmates, but my main fear was not them but my father.

Imagine a wild rabbit being caught and put in a cage. I know what would happen, because a neighbor caught such a rabbit and caged it. All its life that rabbit had had the joy of going where it would, eating what it would, doing what it would without restriction. But suddenly, by the fact that it was caught, its liberty was taken from it by constraint. I saw how the rabbit was afraid of anyone who came near. It would run about within the confines of its cage, seeking a way of escape. After nine days the rabbit killed itself by beating its head against the cage walls. This is the truth; I observed it.

In the same way I had entered into another world—a caged world—and I was desperately trying to find my way out again to freedom. It was not that I was spoiled, as some might think. It was that I was uprooted and placed in a foreign culture. If I had been raised in a cage in the first place, it would have been different. As a free soul I would not have headed for a life of irresponsibility, but rather I would have enjoyed my childhood and then probably spent my days working with agriculture or animal husbandry.

Now I had to find the keys I had lost. I retraced my steps without success. I couldn't find them. My mother's words kept ringing in my ears, "If you don't find the keys, don't come back." She didn't really mean that, of course. She was just being emphatic. But what she unknowingly did was implant an idea in my mind—something I had never thought of before. And at that moment, I resolved to do just that: not go back home where I had to obey people who were strangers.

I still had almost 10 lei on me, so I decided to go see a movie. After that it was nearly 8:00 P.M.—and I headed for the train station. I had never been there, so I didn't know where it was. But I could hear the sounds of trains in the distance, and I tried to follow those sounds.

It was night now, about 10:30 or 11:00 P.M. I met some people, and I told them I wanted to go to Balteni, to my grandmother's. "Where do I catch the train?" They told me that I should follow them and they would get me to the "Gara" (station).

When I saw the Gara from a distance I was elated. When I walked in I was filled with wonder at the size of the place. But at that moment, while I was still marveling at it, some policemen stopped me and asked me what I was doing there. I told them I was going to my grandmother's, but they took me to the police station. They asked my name, address, parents' names, the school I attended and so forth. I told them everything they wanted to know. Actually, my father had drilled all that information into me because he thought I might get lost sometime. The police locked me in a room where, in spite of my being scared, I slept until morning. They woke me about 7:00 A.M., shoved me out onto the street and told me to go home. Instead, I got on a bus and rode all day.

I don't know why my parents didn't search for me. If they had gone to the police they would have found me. Maybe they were afraid of retribution. We were living under strict Communism in those days. But I know the news spread among the neighbors that I had run away, because later in the day, when the bus passed through my neighborhood, some neighbors saw me, ran after the bus, dragged me off and took me home.

Once I was back home, my father gave me a good scolding. I was lucky he didn't beat me but only made me get down on my knees. He had to leave for work right about then, so I got off easy. That was my first time to run away from home—the summer of 1987 when I was seven.

*In my experience, this is a very common phenomenon among abused or disturbed children. They tear apart anything and everything given to amuse them, even bicycles. "Indestructible" toys survive only a short while longer than others. One fifteen-year-old came to our facility because he had taken apart and destroyed almost every appliance in the home, including the family TV.

JMK

CHAPTER 3

Desperate to Escape

That September, school started once again with the same, continuing low grades and resultant scoldings from my father accompanied by beatings. One day I left my pencil box at school. My father railed at me and said, "If you don't find your pencil box tomorrow, don't bother coming home again!" The next morning I went to school and searched, but I couldn't find it. Once again, the idea had been planted in my mind, so I didn't go back home.

I walked about aimlessly a long time. I saw a bicycle unattended, and in spite of not knowing how to ride, I took it. I tried to ride it but kept falling off, so finally I just pushed it, walking down the main street of the city with my school pack on my back. I must have walked five miles with that bicycle. Finally I arrived at the Buzau River and decided I'd had enough. I threw the bicycle down and headed for the bus station, intending somehow to get to my grandmother's house where I felt I belonged.

Once again I wandered around the city quite a bit before finding the bus station. I expected to find a bus that would take me to Balteni, the village where my grandmother lived, but something else awaited me. I was sitting on a bench, my feet barely touching the floor, expecting the bus at any moment, when, to my horror, my father walked into the station. There was no time to hide. He grabbed me, shoved me ahead of him, and we walked home in silence. When we got to the apartment, my father put me at once to studying. I remember falling asleep with a book in my hands.

The next day I ran away again, still hoping I could get to my grandmother's. Again, my father found me. On the way home he pulled on my ear continually and slapped me on the head. I was really beginning to dislike him.

After that, I tried to run away at least once a week. I wanted to be free. I wanted out of my cage. I wanted to be out of the presence of my father. I didn't like school—in fact, I hated it. I wanted to join my classmates in a scheme they cooked up. They got the idea that if they painted the outside of the school with pork fat, the dogs would come and eat the school.

In the autumn of that year (1987) I asked my mother if I could go visit my grandmother. To my surprise she agreed—though she took me herself. Thus I found a better way of getting there than running away. We only stayed a few days, but how I basked in the joy of being in the quiet of the country again and the presence of my grandmother. When it came time to return to the city, I went reluctantly, like a prisoner to the gallows.

Now the problems began in earnest. I had tasted once again the joy of running free. The rabbit was given a few days liberty only to be penned up again. Not only was I that rabbit; I was a caged songbird, too. Once I knew what was outside that cage, I never wanted to be imprisoned again.

In the past when I ran away I had never succeeded in reaching my grandmother because I didn't know the way. Now my mother had done me an inestimable service: She had shown me the bus route.

I started running away more frequently, each time arriving within a few hours at my grandmother's door. I would stay there a few days before my mother came to take me back to the city. When I arrived home, my father would beat me. He always started with his hand and fist. Then he would get a wire cable and beat me on the back until the blood flowed and my back looked as if it had been scourged with a whip.

One time after he finished with the beating, he took me by the ears, lifted me to the ceiling and then knocked me to the floor. He did this twice until blood started flowing from my ears. One had been fractured. When my mother saw my condition and the blood flowing from my ears she started crying and rushed me to the hospital, where I stayed ten days.

After I was discharged from the hospital I ran away again to my grandmother's house. Now I was like a dog that had only one thought—to escape from its captor.

Beaten again and again, I focused only on my primary goal and ignored the beatings.

After a week with my grandmother, my mother came to take me home. On the way back to the city, for some reason my mother gave me her purse to carry. When we arrived in the city I walked in silence with my mother from the bus stop toward home, knowing what awaited me. Arriving at our apartment building, we entered the dark hallway and made our way up the three flights of stairs. Once again instinct took over. The instant my mother put the key in the lock I ran, leaping over several steps at a time in my haste to get to the exit and as far away from there as I could.

I went first to a park, where I was shocked to see my father coming toward me, materializing out of nowhere like a monster in a nightmare. Noticing the purse in my hand, he asked me where I was going. I told him I was going to buy some matches. The lie didn't go, and he took me home. He was riding a bicycle and made me run ahead of the bicycle. At home I got another beating.

The same year, in the apartment building where we lived on the third floor was a family of Gypsies. That family was engaged in witchcraft. The woman liked my father because he was a well-built man and handsome, and his behavior outside the home was exemplary. No one would ever guess how cruel he was, beating his child almost daily to the point of insensibility. So, the Gypsy woman put a death curse on my mother. She placed some eggs at the door to our apartment with the expectation that my mother would touch them and receive the curse. But my father found them, smashed them and threw them outside in the garbage.

Once again the Gypsy woman put eggs at our door, but this time I found them, picked them up and put them in the garbage "inside" our apartment. Thus, the curse passed to me, carrying with it the worst terror of my life.

It started, like so many other times, with my running away to my grandmother's and my mother coming to get me. To go home, we had to take the train to Buzau and then a bus. This time my heart was pounding with fear the entire trip. When we climbed the stairs to our apartment the fear intensified—until it finally turned into panic.

When we arrived at the apartment I was sent to take a bath and change my clothes. Then the terror started.

In those days my father was always drunk, though it didn't really show. This particular afternoon he drank a glass of cognac and afterward started downing beers. After he got worked up he took me into my bedroom, where he tied my hands with a rope and then fastened the rope to the wall with nails. He left me there while he went to eat and finish drinking his beer. Meanwhile, he sent my younger brother Georgica to take me a glass of beer, which I drank. I stood there, nailed to the wall, and waited. I had no idea of what I was in for.

The beating that day lasted four hours. My father beat me with his hands and fists, kicked me with his feet, strapped me with his belt—and afterward struck me repeatedly with an iron rod. He hit me everywhere: head, hands, abdomen, back, feet and in the groin. It was horrible—atrocious. I was only nine years old.

The day after, I could eat only with difficulty. When I tried to use the toilet, something was wrong. When I examined myself I found my entire private region was purple and swollen. My face was also black and blue and swollen. When my mother saw my condition, she took me to the hospital, where I was confined two weeks. I received an injection every six hours. Meanwhile, my condition was reported to the police, who came to the hospital to investigate. They looked me over "everywhere." They were stunned at what they saw. My father was arrested and taken in for interrogation. In those days, a citizen who made an offhand remark against the government could spend years in prison, but in this case, my father was only required to make a declaration that he would never beat me again—which he subsequently ignored.

While I was in the hospital, my mother went to a witch to find out if I was cursed. The witch told my mother the whole story about the Gypsy woman. I must state emphatically that these curses are no idle superstition. They work through calling on the powers of darkness and have power against the unsuspecting. More people are affected by them than they realize. Not only the Gypsies engage in that dark trade. Many of the Orthodox priests are known for their willingness to place curses for a fee. But sometimes, like poison gas propelled in the wrong direction by a contrary current of wind or a venomous serpent sent slithering down the wrong path, these curses go astray. Thus, the curse passing to me provoked a rage in my father that ended with me in the hospital. However, this curse ended with a bizarre twist. During the exact time my father was savagely beating me, the Gypsy woman fell sick. Her liver ruptured, and she died on the spot.

After that, the most brutal beating of my life, my parents decided to put *me* in a mental hospital. They said *I* must be crazy. I stayed in the mental hospital two weeks. The staff asked me a lot of questions and gave me a medical exam. Their conclusion was that I was completely normal. My parents put me in that place twice. Actually, I didn't mind it at all. I was free while I was in there and didn't have to see my father. Because I had been interned in a psychiatric hospital, however, many colleagues in my class and the kids around where I lived called me names and made fun of me. They called me "Nebunul" (the crazy one). That name even followed me later to Bucharest.

That summer of 1988 I stayed home instead of running away to my grandmother; during those days my fourth brother was born. Speaking of births, for me birthdays never meant a thing. They didn't exist. Never once did I have a birthday party or any presents. Never once did my father say, "Happy birthday!" The day was just like any other.

Only once do I remember an exception. Just before my birthday I knew that my mother had bought two storybooks for me. Later, I saw my father reading them—and then I never saw them again.

In the fall of 1988, a few days short of my tenth birthday, I started third grade. One afternoon on the way home from school I got the idea of running away again—but this time I intended to run away to my paternal grandparents. I don't know why. I had little to do with them. My grandfather was responsible for my father's condition, and my grandmother was not that warm, either. I headed for the bus station, but I didn't know which bus to take. It got to be nearly 11:00 o'clock at night, and I was still in the city, wandering about. I found myself outside a bookstore. In the time of Ceausescu, bookstores sold not only books, but also notebooks, painting canvases, toys and a variety of things. The bookstore was dark and the windows and door covered with gratings. I stopped a bit to look, attracted by the covers of the books on display. Impulsively, I picked up a stone and broke a window. I found a stick inside the window about a meter long. I used it to knock two or three books into my hands and started to read. One was a book with pictures, which I enjoyed immensely. Relaxing, I hunkered down next to the broken window and continued to read.

Meanwhile, a car with four policemen came roaring up the street at high speed to investigate. When they saw me, they looked at me as if I were crazy. They took me to a precinct station—one I had never been to before. I was afraid, but I managed to keep my fear under control until morning when my mother came and got me.

My mother had to go to work every day at 2:00 P.M., and my father didn't come home from his job until 4:00. During those two hours I was alone. I felt free after my mother left, but about 3:00 o'clock I would begin feeling a sense of impending doom—the anticipation of my father's arrival an hour hence. The closer it came to 4:00 o'clock the worse I felt until the moment when my father put the key in the door and my heart began to pound.

My father was often tired from work. He would go into his room, close the door and go to sleep. When he got up later, I knew the potential for trouble. Immediately I looked for something to do—anything. I would get down on the floor and start picking lint from the carpet, or I would fold clothes, wash the floor or dust.

When I came from school I would walk as slowly as possible. Anytime I brought home grades of 4 or less I knew that I faced giving an account of it to my father. Many other times, knowing my father would arrive at 4:00, I would go to bed myself at 3:00 and sleep so that when he came in he wouldn't bother me.

The day after the bookstore incident, I was enjoying once again my two hours of afternoon quiet. Nevertheless, many thoughts were tumbling through my head, especially what I faced at 4:00 o'clock when my nemesis put the key in the door. On impulse, I undid the door, slipped out into the hallway—and was gone.

Being more familiar now with the bus routes, I headed for my beloved grandmother's house. I passed a few pleasant days there until my mother heard where I was and came to get me.

I stayed home about a month after that, but I was biding my time—perhaps building up my reserves for an even greater adventure, for it was during those days the idea first entered my head to go to Bucharest. I was getting tired of the pattern that had developed: running to my grandmother's, staying a few days, my mother coming to get me, returning to Buzau, my father beating me—I needed something new. I was old enough now to be aware that Romania extended beyond the boundaries of Buzau and my grandparents' farms. There was a huge city out there just waiting to be explored.

So I got on a train going to Bucharest. I duped the conductor by saying I was going to visit my grandmother but had lost all my money.

CHAPTER 4

The Train Station

I found Bucharest larger and more exciting than I could have imagined. It was once called "The Paris of the East." There was even an Arch of Triumph. I thought it was a beautiful city—though tourists considered it shabby and rundown from years of neglect. Ceausescu had concocted the grandiose scheme of making Bucharest the showpiece of the socialist world. In a matter of days a couple of square kilometers in the center of the city were bulldozed, and the bewildered, dispossessed inhabitants were left to fend for themselves. Residences, historic buildings, churches—nothing escaped the relentless bulldozers. A huge square was carved out, then a boulevard extending two miles. The square was destined for a monumental, white marble edifice: a display of megalomania to rival any in history. The Palace of the People would contain a thousand rooms. It would be the largest building in Europe.

Food and natural resources were exported to pay for this monument to Ceausescu's madness. So, while the public went without food and electricity, enormous chandeliers comprised of thousands of bulbs were installed in the Palace. Interestingly, the chief architect for this monolith was a woman not yet thirty years old.

The boulevard was to rival the Parisian Champs d' Elysees. Luxury stores and apartment blocks faced with white marble lined the boulevard on either side while fountains sprayed water into the air. (Actually, by Western standards, it was gaudy.) The apartments were, of course, destined for the use of the Communist elite. Though the scheme was an imitation of the French, the French concepts of liberty, equality and fraternity were conspicuously absent. So while this monumental construction project was underway, the rest of Bucharest decayed.

The capital was too huge a city to be explored by foot as I had done in Buzau. Of course, I didn't know anyone or the city, so I stayed in the area right around the Gara de Nord (North Station). I ate from the garbage bins and slept in the depot waiting rooms.

The Gara de Nord is an L-shaped building that would probably be attractive if it were colored something other than gray. The shorter leg is nothing more than an elongated passageway, with miscellaneous rooms on either side, leading straight ahead to the twelve train platforms. The longer leg is perpendicular to the shorter, so the end of one is also the end of the other. The longer leg extends about 300 feet (100 meters) in all, with an exit at both ends. At the end with the platforms are a couple small food shops where the boy prostitutes wait. As one proceeds toward the other exit, the passageway becomes more complex. There are several food shops and a waiting room. A doorway to the right opens into a large foyer with ticket windows off to one side and another exit ahead. Back in the main corridor there is another passageway out of the building to the left, and just before the main exit to the street is an escalator leading down into another long passageway going to the metro station—the subway. This longer leg of the Gara is three stories high and replete with nooks and crannies that the resourceful street child can well make use of. Since some areas must be lit by candle, it is to the children's credit they have not yet burned the place down. When one combines the subway station with the rest of the Gara, there was ample area for the kids to move about. I say "was" because in the last couple years the authorities have attempted to rid the Gara of the presence of every single street child. The entrances are guarded, and if one doesn't have a ticket for a train, one has to pay to get into the building. Even if a kid should have the money, however, he or she would be refused entrance by the guards at the doors.

Some days later, having explored the area around the Gara thoroughly, I hopped a train for Constanta, a port on the Black Sea. I was now determined to explore Romania. It was my first time to view the Black Sea. While viewing the port of Constanta and standing on the shore of the sea, I realized I had already seen more things and been more places than my parents had in their entire lives. I was very happy. Not knowing how the "rules of the street" worked, however, I was picked up by the police in Constanta. They arrested me and took me to the precinct station, where I stayed two days. After that they put me in the juvenile detention center. When I got there, I started crying, saying I wanted to go home. They took all the data on me. As I mentioned, when I was quite small my father taught me everything I needed to know: names, addresses, phone numbers. I stayed in the center seven days, after which my mother came and took me home.

Life in the detention center was very strict. It was completely quiet. We were given enough food and were not beaten. When I arrived at home this time, my father did not beat me.

When all this was happening to me around the ages of eight, nine and ten, I was not thinking at all about the future. My only thought was to stay away from my father. I didn't like him, and I was afraid of him. When I did see him, my only thought was to get as far away from him as I could.

Physically, I resembled my father in appearance, but my heart was with my mother. Whenever I passed people on the street who were suffering, my heart went out to them because that's how my mother was.

I suffered much because of my father. I was always thirsty for affection. During my entire childhood neither my mother nor my father ever hugged me, kissed me or said to me, "Son, we are pleased with you. We are proud of you, and we love you." Perhaps they didn't feel they had anything to be proud of, but after all, I was their son. There must have been something.

I wanted a father-son relationship, but what I got instead was a schoolmaster-student relationship. Every Sunday morning the TV had programs for children, but during those times my father would send me into another room to study. When other kids were allowed to stay out playing in the evenings, I had to come in early to study. I couldn't go out and play soccer without my father giving me a lecture about scuffing my shoes. I couldn't even play on a slide because my father said I would tear my pants. The only thing my father ever did with me that could be considered some kind of recreation was to play cards. Even then, if I beat him and was not humble about it, he would send me to my room to study as punishment.

I was curious about other families, and I watched how other kids lived. I noticed how all my schoolmates carried lunches and had extra money for sweets. I was sent to school without a lunch and had to wait until I got home to eat.

I remember when I was living in the streets in Bucharest, how I would see families together in the park. I would approach the children and ask to play with them. (Remember I was just a young boy, nine or ten years old.) Despite my appearance, they often let me. But all the time we were playing, I was thinking of how after we played they would go home to a nice bed and I would go to sleep in the musty basement of the Gara or in the drafty stairway of an apartment building.

My mother was different. She didn't care about the grades I brought home from school. What was important to her was only that I passed. So she was not in agreement with the beatings my father administered, but in first grade she didn't intervene at all. When I got bigger, my mother tried to intervene. Sometimes she would rescue me from my father's beatings, but other times she would get beaten herself or shut out on the balcony.

My question was, Why was my father so severe? Why couldn't we have a normal, healthy family? Going back into my father's past, I observed that he did not participate in the affection and love of his parents. On top of that, when he was only fourteen he had to leave home to find his way in the world. When he married, the entire wedding gift he received was a quilt and a pillow even though his parents had the money to have given something better. My mother observed that anytime my father was in the presence of his father, he was stiff. He too was on guard.

From 1988 to 1989 I ran away several times from home—so many I will forgo detailing each one. That was the time I began to try to understand the world—how to survive in it. In those times, the only way I had of getting food was to eat leftovers and scraps. The only place I had to sleep was the waiting room of the Gara.

Often, the police would arrest me, call my parents and then put me back out on the street. So many times my mother was called to travel to another city to get me, but when she got there, I was nowhere to be found. During these same years, I learned how to avoid and escape from the police. I remember the time I was arrested and taken to the main police station in Slobozia, where I stayed two days. Since no one was watching me, I sneaked out of the building and went over a fence. I was very pleased at having accomplished my escape and felt that I had learned something.

In May 1989 I was arrested again in Constanta, and I found myself in the detention center. After my mother came to get me, I stayed at home awhile and finished third grade. But when summer came, I felt the wanderlust again.

One day I discovered where my father kept his money. It was two thousand lei, his month's salary and a very large sum in those days. I was supposed to be watching my little brothers, but after my father left for work I took the money, two bags of clothes and ran off, leaving my brothers alone in the apartment.

On the way to the train station I stopped to buy some cigarettes and then continued on to the station, where I bought a ticket to Bucharest. It was the first time I was actually traveling with a valid ticket, so I was proud of it. On the way to Bucharest I made friends with two runaway boys on the train who were bigger than I. Upon arrival in Bucharest we went to a movie together: *Rocky II*. When we left the theater I discovered I was missing fifteen hundred lei. I remonstrated with my new pals, but they feigned innocence, so there was nothing I could do but go my own way. I now had only four hundred lei left from the two thousand. I headed for the Gara de Nord, where other kids saw that I had money and took it from me by force. Nevertheless, I was not upset because I made friends with them.

A few days later I was arrested and taken to the detention center in Bucharest. I was dirty and full of lice. After they took the information from me, they put me in the charge of two older boys. They took me to get a bath and a haircut, but then started hitting me with broomsticks and chopped my hair with scissors.

The portions of food were very small. For breakfast we got one piece of bread with jam; for lunch we got about 100 grams (4 ounces) of food with two pieces of bread; and in the evening we got tea and macaroni. Being already underfed, the portions they gave were not enough.

In the daytime they put us all together in a large room. The older boys could watch television and play chess, but we smaller boys had to just sit on hard chairs all day with nothing to do except be quiet. Some boys made dice from bread and used them to gamble. If anyone made any noise, the big boys beat them. If the room was noisy and wouldn't quiet down, everyone was made to put their heads under the chairs and sleep. In that same detention center, older boys who had done something serious in breaking the law were put together with younger street kids. To my happiness I stayed there only two days. Once again, my mother came to take me home. When I arrived home my father didn't beat me because when he saw the lacerations on my head from the beating I got in the detention center, he said I had had enough.

Seeing that they had so many problems with me, my mother decided to put me in a correctional institution. They had enough reason, inasmuch as I had stolen the two thousand lei and my theft had left the family without enough money for food. But first, they took me back to the psychiatric hospital. During the time I was shut up in there, the police did the paperwork to send me to the

correctional school, but my mother began to think better of her decision and realized that it would be the greatest mistake of their lives. My mother knew someone in
the police department and asked that the dossier be
destroyed. So, I escaped.

CHAPTER 5

The Revolution

After everything that happened to me in 1989, I stayed home for a while and made a decision never to leave again.

During that year my little sister, Mihaela, was born.

Being yet a child, I had no political opinions. I was not awaiting the day when Romania would escape the Communist tyranny. My father always said that Ceausescu was our "daddy" and we should love him. In spite of that, my parents did not appreciate the Communist system.

The winter of 1989 was especially harsh with regard to living conditions. The winter holiday season was approaching when people traditionally feasted, but we had not a scrap extra in the house. There was no food in the marketplace to be had. My mother stood in line two days to buy meat, but she returned home empty handed. By the time she reached the head of the line, only bones, with barely a shred of meat on them, were left, and they were not worth bringing home.

Electricity was turned off several hours a day, and only enough heat circulated in the radiators to keep the room temperature at 50° or 55° F (10°–13° C). There were those who were plunged into such despair at these conditions they contemplated suicide. Even some Christians, who should have had their faith to sustain them, thought that God had abandoned them. They understood what Job's wife meant when she advised her suffering husband to curse God and die.

Tyranny eventually runs its course. In the week before Christmas my mother began to hear talk from the neighbors of unrest in the city of Timisoara. Citizens there were in open revolt against the government. The pent-up frustrations of years exploded as the populace gathered in the public square and shouted in defiance of the Communists, "God exists! God exists! God exists!"

Even though news was censored, word began to spread like smoke from a grass fire. It was rumored that tanks had moved into the city, fired on the people and many were killed. When I heard about it I was scared that the same would happen in our city. I was afraid of dying.

On December 21 and 22 the unrest shifted to Bucharest. If the weather had been normal for December with snow and ice, the Revolution probably could not have succeeded. But people considered it a miracle from God when the temperature on those two winter days was spring-like.

Ceausescu, aware of the civil unrest in Timisoara, made

a speech in one of the public squares of Bucharest from high up on a balcony. If one didn't understand Romanian, the man appeared impressive. His powerful gestures and forceful way of speaking could stir a crowd. Actually, he wasn't saying anything—only a series of trite, hackneyed phrases strung together, typical of Communist rhetoric. But the crowd that day was in a bad mood, wanting something more tangible than banality.

Ceausescu was not so much smart as he was cunning. He sensed his speech was not going across, so in an attempt to appease the populace, he offered an increase in salaries. Instead of placating the people, his offer only showed his weakness; at once the crowd surged toward the building from which he was speaking. His wife, Elena, sensing something disastrous but not knowing quite what, shouted at her husband, "What's happening? Is it an earthquake?"

"Shut up!" he snapped.

Orders were given to fire on the crowd. At first, many were killed—but then the soldiers refused to continue. Ordered again to shoot, the soldiers pointed their weapons into the air and fired. The upper stories of many buildings still bear the scars of that day.

Ceausescu, together with his wife, Elena, took flight from the city in a helicopter. Since there were escape tunnels under the city, this was a grave mistake. He thought he was fleeing to safety—but his time had come. A tyrant can hold the people with bread, but when there is no more bread, his tedious weaknesses become conspicuous and adulation turns to contempt.

Not far from Bucharest the helicopter pilot set down on a country highway, opened the door and pushed the rattled dictator and his wife out onto the road. Only a few minutes before, he had been addressing a hundred thousand people in the public square. Now the man who had had the power of life and death over millions, who thought his people would always worship him as a god, stood by the side of the road and hitchhiked like a vagabond drifter. A Romanian-made Dacia came along and picked the disconcerted couple up. Before long, however, they ran into a roadblock. The police took over from there. They were taken to a military facility and imprisoned. Brought up before a hastily convened court, they were condemned to death. Elena Ceausescu began to cajole, speaking in a hurt tone to the soldiers guarding her. "Why? What is the meaning of this? I was always a mother to you boys."

One of the young soldiers replied sullenly, "You're not my mother."

Now Elena Ceausescu, who had presented herself before the governments of the world as a woman of refinement and culture (though she never made it beyond fourth grade), began to curse and swear. Her husband, Nicolae, protested that he did not recognize the authority of the court. He could have saved his breath. On Christmas morning the fallen despot, who in his youth had declared when he could not learn a trade that he would be the Stalin of Romania—he and his foul-mouthed wife were shot by a firing squad. The damage he did to Romania will take decades to erase.

Once Ceausescu left Bucharest, the radio and TV began to carry reports of the unimaginable events. As a family, we sat before the TV hardly believing what we saw, but still without hope that the Revolution would prevail or that the Communist regime would fall. I grasped little of the reality of what we saw. I was only afraid that the disruptive events would somehow touch our family and we would incur punishment—though we had done nothing. Like most, I had a fear of the Communists and their system.

But the Revolution achieved its goals: The people prevailed. December 22 would forever be remembered as a new day for Romania just as July 4 is for the United States.

A new government was quickly established. The electricity was turned on, the heat was turned up, and food was rushed to the stores. Adults who had never seen a banana thought they were to be eaten with the skin on.

People hastened to celebrate Christmas in total freedom for the first time in decades. In the following days my father even wanted to go out into the streets holding a placard with the name of the revolutionary party written on it to express his new freedom to do so.

After the Revolution, things settled down—though it would be a long time before matters could be called normal. The people had to recover from years of oppression. Some were quite bitter. The police who had behaved high-handedly and often with cruelty were now cowering in their precinct stations—it would be a year before they ventured out much. Meanwhile, police teams were moved in their entirety from one precinct to another with anonymity to avoid retaliation from citizens who hadn't appreciated being harassed, tortured or imprisoned unjustly. Many former members of the secret police were beaten in the streets.

After having lived for years in isolation, people were now free to travel. The reactions of many when visiting countries to the west were touching. Upon walking into prosperous, well-stocked stores, they stood and wept, saying, "Look what Ceausescu did to us."

Though food and other goods were now more abundant, shortages of some basic items still prevailed for a time. Then a new scourge: Inflation set in. The communists had guaranteed every adult a job, and now that guarantee was no longer good. Massive construction projects employing thousands stopped dead along with Ceausescu. The lights went out on his showcase boulevard; the half-finished apartments, with their empty window sockets gaping, looked for all the world like ancient Roman ruins.

Romania began to look to the rest of the world for humanitarian aid, and it began to arrive. I remember my parents coming back from work with clothes and shoes for us that had been given by some charitable organization. Nevertheless, instead of being happy with what they received they were in a snit because the distribution had not been carried out equitably. Some of the higher ups took more than their share. (That still goes on.)

I started back to school, and it went all right. My father was not quite as strict as he had been and stopped riding me about my homework. Nevertheless, his attitude toward me was of contempt for a vagabond. His demeanor toward me was cold. I could not feel that I was his son and surely my fear of him did not diminish.

I didn't fare much better with the neighborhood. The older people looked upon me as an aberration that would, perhaps, contaminate their children. As for the kids themselves, some enjoyed hearing me tell stories of my wanderings. Others considered me some kind of criminal.

When my father fought with my mother, I preferred to go study for school or to stay a half hour in the bathroom. My mother thought of getting a divorce, but she had nowhere to go, and she had five children to take care of.

I finally finished fourth grade; and vacation, the student's respite, began. I had a lot more freedom during vacation. My parents would let me play outdoors without too many restrictions. I often went walking in the city with my brothers from 9:00 in the morning until 9:00 at night. We came home only to eat some lunch around 2:00 P.M., and then we went back out again to get away from my father. We were happy whenever he left for work.

In September of 1990 I started fifth grade. I had to study French and German that year, and I didn't like it at all. I remember one day getting a grade of 3 in German and coming home in fear of another beating from my father. That day I said the Lord's Prayer one hundred and three times, hoping it would help. I fell asleep saying it. To my amazement, the next morning when my father looked over my schoolwork and saw the grade of 3 he said nothing. He did, however, put me to reading German lessons, but since he did not know German and had no way of knowing what I was really doing, I got by easier.

Inasmuch as I had more homework in fifth grade, my

father put me to studying four or five hours a day. So that he would leave me in peace, I sat in the kitchen until late studying or sometimes just thinking. After he went to bed, I would, too.

During the 1990–1991 school year I did not have any great conflicts with my father. The reason was that he didn't know fifth grade material very well and, thus, couldn't judge my efforts.

The same year, 1990–1991, many left Romania to go work in other countries. There was a neighbor who worked in construction who wanted to take me along with him to Germany. He told me I should study German well in school because it would be an advantage. I was disappointed when he left for Germany and did not take me along.

After I finished fifth grade in June 1991, I decided to spend the summer working on a farm. I worked the entire summer—all the way to the middle of September. It was hard, but I found some pride in working shoulder to shoulder with the men. I was only eleven years old, but I had to carry 100-pound sacks of grain and get out in the fields and hoe just as fast as the others. I worked long and hard, but to my disappointment, when I got home, my parents took all the money I had earned. I was able to buy only two shirts and a pair of blue jeans; I never saw the rest.

Another time I had earned a little money and bought my first watch. My father scolded me about it and took it away.

In front of our apartment building was a game table. Lots of men would gamble there and send me to buy cigarettes for them. I picked up some spare change this way, so I was not entirely without money.

That fall I started sixth grade. In those days the street kid phenomenon had exploded, and there were programs on TV disclosing the problem to the public. To my surprise I recognized many of the children shown. The documentaries also told how a limited number of organizations were springing up to help the children. After watching, I began to miss the streets.

CHAPTER 6

The Reason for Street Children

The phenomenon of the street child, which exploded numerically in 1990, had its origin in the Communist regime. Dictator Nicolae Ceausescu not only encouraged but demanded that every family consist of five children in order to increase the work force of Romania. He offered incentives such as salary increases according to the number of children in a family.

However, the reality was that the salary increase did not cover the expenses of additional children. People had no experience managing large families, and the Communist regime gave them no other help. Many families simply ran out of money and living space. Faced with the inability to care for their children and a disintegrating familial environment, many opted to put one or more of their children in an orphanage. The orphanages, in turn, became crowded and the children subjected to indignities no child should have to endure. There was little supervision. At mealtimes, the older children took food off the plates of the younger ones, who then went hungry. The younger children were also subject to bullying and battering by the older ones. With a shortage of beds, two were made to sleep in a bed made for one. Putting two pubescent boys together in such a situation who were just awakening sexually spawned an increase in the homosexual population. And when two boys in a bed were finished with each other, they prowled the poorly supervised dormitories for other victims to seduce. The children were mistreated physically and mentally by both inmates and staff. They were beaten, slapped around, shouted at, insulted and cursed. And when they had had enough, many escaped, pouring out into the streets. Whatever the conditions were on the streets, they were preferable to where they had been. When the police arrested such children, their solution was to take them back to the orphanages they came from.

I knew many kids who had fled the orphanages, but among them were also older boys who told of being shoved out onto the streets when they turned eighteen. And there they were, legally adults but without a trade, without a place to live, without anything. The only possibility they had of a home was the Gara.

Many families, not having money with which to care for their children, sent the children out to beg or to steal. Thus, another type of street child came into existence: the market child.

Market children were those who left home early in the

morning and headed for the marketplaces where they begged or stole fruit, vegetables, billfolds, purses—whatever they could. At night they gathered together once again at their hovels and shared their take of the day. Some of them gained more in a day than an honest laborer, but they tended to be wasteful of what they had and lived only from one day to the next.

Often, kids of this class would be arrested by the police, taken to the station and from there to the Center for Minors. Their parents would be notified, and they would come and take the children home.

Thus, many of those children began activities that would eventually take them to prison. They were the professional thieves of tomorrow.

Another group out on the streets were those who had run away from home. I was in that category. Because of mistreatment and lack of parental love, many decided to leave home. Among them were many who had lived in rural areas where the conditions were horrible. From the time they were little they had been put at hard agricultural labor working in the fields or caring for animals. They fled home to obtain freedom. Plenty of those who left home after the Revolution of December 1989 did so because they saw special programs on television about runaway children. Although the public might be shocked at the life of a street child, to a child who was panting for freedom from harsh conditions, such a life was indeed inviting. Thus, because of the witless way in which their parents treated them, they resolved their problems by fleeing.

In some cases, children, instead of running away, were

put out on the streets by their parents. Sometimes this was because the child was causing problems and the parents had no idea how to cope or deal with them. In other cases, they simply did not have enough money and decided to get rid of one or more of their kids.

Whatever, in the time of Ceausescu, the street child situation was much more under control than after the Revolution. The Communist regime had no system of social programs to deal with such problems. Their method of dealing with street kids was to take them back to their families or, if the family could not be found, to take them to an orphanage. The police were very strict with children. If the police saw a child in the streets at night, they would immediately begin questioning and asking for identity documents. (Children fourteen and older were required to carry documents.) If none could be produced, the child was escorted to the precinct station. It was very rare that they let one out easily. After the Revolution, things got better. There was much more freedom to be out on the streets as basic human rights were restored to the populace. About the same time, organizations began to appear that were concerned with street children.

CHAPTER 7

Dangers in the Streets

I was now eleven and a half—about to leave childhood and enter adolescence. I had already had many more experiences than the average Romanian child, but I did not feel fulfilled or satisfied. I wanted something else out of life. For one thing, I was thirsty for affection and didn't get it from anyone.

It was now that I began to think of the future. I saw the financial problems my parents were having, and I didn't want to be like them. I saw how hard they worked, but that they did not even have job security under the new regime. Many workers had been let go, and my parents were continually afraid it would happen to them, too. As for me, I could not imagine working in a factory the rest of my life. I wanted something different but didn't know what. What else was there?

Restless, I left home again in October 1991 after my

twelfth birthday. I went to Bucharest with the idea of seeing "what's new" around the Gara. Upon arrival, I met some of the boys I had known when I was there back in 1988. I was really glad to see them again after such a long time. I jumped right into gang life, started sniffing aurolac and made my "home" with them. We slept in a corner above the room where the mail was brought in off the trains. It was a horrible place. Often postal workers would beat us up in the process of trying to drive us out. We didn't like the police one bit either.

The police were a major problem for the street kids. I remember especially one incident when I was about nine or ten and had run away from home to Bucharest. I had spent the evening riding around in a trolley bus. I fell asleep, and when I awoke, I was somewhere near the garage where the buses were parked for the night. I had no idea where I was. I asked a man how I could get to the Gara. I fell into conversation with him and told him my story—how I had run away from home—the whole thing. He was a nice man and gave me one hundred lei ($1.60). After leaving him I ran into a squad of police. They wanted to haul me off with them, but I gave them a big sob story of how I was tired of living on the streets and really wanted to go home. I don't think I convinced them, but at that moment they were called to some emergency and let me go.

I walked on toward the Gara and ran into yet another squad. It wasn't my lucky night. Even though I told them I had already been interrogated by another patrol and let go, they took me in anyhow. When we arrived at the precinct there were about thirty other kids who had been arrested. In the morning, I gave the one hundred lei to the police to buy bread for the whole crowd. In reality, I was having fun. We street kids didn't have much to occupy our attention, and an arrest was a distraction. My sense of having fun lasted until a group of police entered the room where we were held and started beating all of us, one after the other. I was the first. I got four blows on the back, legs, stomach—wherever. After that, they took us all out into a corridor and put us on our knees with our arms raised into the air. If anyone complained, he was beaten with an even larger stick—something like a baseball bat.

We stayed on our knees in the corridor until everyone was beaten, and then we were led toward the exit. As we approached the exit, policemen were lined up on either side of the hallway. As we passed between them they kicked us. In spite of all I had gone through in there, all I could think of was that I was free.

On the first floor of the Gara was a place where bundles of newspapers were distributed. Many times they found several bundles missing, and the guilt fell on us because we were nearby, though we had nothing to do with it. Because of several similar conflicts, it seemed as if it was getting harder for me to live in the Gara, so I moved to the port city of Constanta on the Black Sea. Once there, I began to investigate the various areas of the city where I might sleep: apartment buildings, the naval museum and the bushes. Then I started stealing whatever I needed to make me comfortable.

I didn't want to sleep in the Constanta Gara because the

police patrolled the place thoroughly and were very strict just like in Ceausescu's time. Once they caught me and beat me on the palms of my hands with their truncheons until my hands were swollen and I couldn't stand anymore. Their method worked, because after that I stayed out of the Gara.

In the tourist area of Constanta I found an old boat and hid out there. One day the boat was gone and my clothes with it.

Around the same time a man invited me to stay at his place. Since it was autumn and getting cold outside, I decided to take him up on it. He had given me his address, so I hopped a bus for the forty-kilometer trip to the town of Ovidiu. When I arrived it was late, and the man had me undress and get into bed. To my surprise he turned out to be a homosexual. I was shocked and frightened at how he wanted to use me. I tried to just go to sleep, but spurred on by his lust, he kept waking me up. I emphatically refused each time. Finally I began to complain bitterly and threaten that I would report him to the police. Having no success, he threw me out on the street at 5:00 o'clock in the morning.

I had other similar experiences—an old watchman once tried to force me—but I stood my ground. I had no inclinations toward that kind of sexual activity. It was fortunate for me that I already had an interest in girls, otherwise I might have fallen into the trap of homosexuality just as so many other boys did.

I found it hard living in Constanta. I ate scraps from tables and begged in order to survive, but people were not generous like they were in Bucharest. Seeing that I was in desperate straits and it was now the middle of winter, I decided to return home. I finally arrived in Buzau after going through a number of difficulties. Among them, I was thrown off a train in a location where I had not the least idea of where I was and had to walk thirty kilometers to the next station. It was February and cold, but I was pretty tough for a twelve-year-old.

After all that, when I arrived at the apartment my father would not let me in. I told him I was sorry and that I would change, but he wouldn't listen. After my father had left for work, my mother took me to the barbershop, then back home where she set out clean clothes—and put me to bed. Somehow she convinced my father to take me back.

In the spring of 1992 the situation between my father and me grew even worse. We talked very little, and when we did he was very formal and distant. I felt disconnected from the family. My thoughts turned once again to the streets. Pure and simple, I just could not live with my parents.

All this time there continued a yearning in me for a normal family. That was not extinguished. I would observe a family walking together along the street: father, mother and children. I would begin to fantasize about being part of such a happy group. But it was only fantasy, and the conflicts continued.

Sometimes my father would be obvious in his discrimination between my brothers and me. One day at the table, one of my brothers offered me a piece of meat, which another brother wanted. He went to my father and told him I had taken it from him by force. My father came, took my plate of food and broke it over my head. Blood poured from my scalp. I will bear the scar to my grave.

Increasingly unhappy, I decided to leave again. I waited until taking an important test in May 1992 so I could get credit for the school year, and then I left.

I went first to Constanta. Since it was summer, the tourist areas of the city were crowded. I stayed most of the summer there. There were not many things to occupy myself with in Constanta, so I made my own program. In the mornings I would go to the coffee shops and bakeries where I ate leftover scraps. Then I would go and beg until around 3:00 or 4:00 in the afternoon. After that I would relax at the beach or go see a movie. I began to know the city quite well. At that time, there were no organizations working with street children, so one had to survive on one's own. At night I slept in the bushes. I put down a piece of cardboard and "went to bed." Many times I was roused by the police and taken for interrogation. They would usually let me go after I promised to go back home—but not always. Sometimes I had to escape from them.

With lots of time on my hands, there wasn't a film in town that I hadn't seen. I kept up with everything new that came along.

I stayed in Constanta until August when I left for Bucharest. Right away I met with my old gang, and they welcomed me back. There were many, many more kids in the gang now than there had been the previous year.

Meanwhile, they had moved their sleeping quarters to a basement room in the Gara where old records were stored. Old registers from the years going back to 1960 were thrown down there—and that's where we slept. I entered into their routine at once. The only thing I had to adjust to was being in a gang with organization. We had to pool our money to buy drugs and candles (since there were no light bulbs down there). It was all simple if one just had the brains to know how to survive.

I liked to stay drugged there in the Gara until it was time to go out and rustle up some money. With the money, I would buy aurolac, cigarettes and go see the latest movie.

One of the most visible signs of the liberty of the street kids is the cigarette in the mouth. I didn't know a single street kid that didn't smoke. We were addicted more to cigarettes than to aurolac. If we woke in the night, having smoked all we had, we went out looking for butts. The best place to find them was between the train tracks and the platforms. Any time we were arrested and kept locked up for any length of time, we wanted cigarettes more than food.

Sometimes our gang would leave the Gara for a couple of days because we were under constant stress over the possibility of the police harassing us. The police knew where we were sleeping and often paid us visits. They would spray something like mace into the air. I would stuff a rag in my mouth as a filter to breathe through and shut my eyes tight because it burned. Many police did this for amusement.

CHAPTER 8

Getting Food

I had a variety of ways to get money or find food to eat. In the mornings I used to sell newspapers with another boy named Adrian. There was a man who had a newsstand near the Gara, and in order to sell his papers more quickly, he would give us a bundle to take and sell in other areas. We didn't make any money selling the papers themselves because we couldn't charge more than the established price, but often people would give us a tip, and we made money that way.

In the Gara were some restaurants where we went and ate what was left on the tables. We would also go out on the platforms and beg food from people who were eating there. Within a few blocks of the Gara were other restaurants where we would go and snatch scraps from the tables and sometimes drinks.

My main method of making money was to go into the

center of the city where there were many theaters, coffee-houses and other such establishments where I begged from the customers.

In Bucharest we would write an announcement on a piece of paper or cardboard. It would go like this:

TESTIMONIAL

We beg of you to help Catalin Dobrisan with some money so he can obtain food and clothing because he is destitute. He is cared for by an elderly couple over eighty years of age.

Thank you for your help!

At the bottom was a seal that looked rather official if one didn't examine it too closely. It was done placing a five-lei coin under the paper and rubbing a pencil over it or stamping the impression into the paper. The finishing touch was a signature by whoever could scribble one and make it look impressive.

The placard was put inside a clear plastic bag, and, with this in hand, I would go from car to car throughout a train. It goes without saying I would start with the first class cars where the people with money were riding.

I would always plan my trips—first, to be on trains where I knew there would be a good chance of picking up money, and second, so that I could get back to Bucharest in the evening in time to take in a movie.

Going from compartment to compartment in the trains, some people would give me food, others money, while others would simply ignore me or turn their heads away. Some asked me questions, and, of course, I gave them a hard-luck story that was pretty much lies. Sometimes I returned from a jaunt with nothing, and that left me rather despondent.

Christmas always brought a sure measure of success. We would go through the subway trains singing Christmas carols. There was a lot of competition: Little kids, big kids and other groups of people came into the city from rural areas attired in traditional Romanian dress. I would go into a subway car, station myself in the middle and sing. After my song, I would go from person to person, my hand extended palm up. Some would give me money, but there were always those who turned their heads. There were some street kids who rode the subway trains and sang from morning until night every day.

Another method was to go begging in the restaurants and coffeehouses. I went a lot into the center of Bucharest where there were many restaurants. I would go from one table to another, asking kindly if they might not help me so I could buy a little bread or food. Often the owner would run us out. That didn't deter us, since we just waited outside until the diners exited and then begged them for money.

If after two hours I hadn't collected a thing I would get very impatient. I would start to curse and swear and hate those who ignored my condition. Other times, I would stand and look wistfully through the window at those who were dining in an attempt to inspire pity for me. Nevertheless, more times than not, all these ploys produced nothing and I went away hungry and disheartened.

I could usually depend more on coffeehouses. They

wouldn't allow me to enter, but if I stood by the door I could usually pick up some change. On the rare occasions when I did get into one of those places, I would usually leave with something. After the diners left, if I got to a table before the waiter, there was usually quite a bit of leftover food and drink.

The restaurants were different. The waiter was at the table the instant the diners left. I was not of a mind to try to get to the table ahead of him, so I chose to wait outside for whatever I could get.

Another possibility was to wait outside a theater at the box office. I would accost people and say I wanted to see the film but didn't have enough money. Often I was able to collect a lot more than the price of a ticket.

What for me was one of the more exhausting methods was to stand at the exit of a subway station on the stairs with a little box, asking passersby for money. On a good day I could get quite a bit. But the main thing required was patience and enduring the cold and wind. The steps were very cold.

More than any other place, the handicapped children gathered in the subway stations to beg. Many had twisted limbs or withered hands; sometimes by hiding their limb, they were able to give the impression it was missing altogether.

People often gave not so much out of pity but out of a religious incentive. In other words, the act of charity would benefit not so much the child as the giver, who would thereby achieve some measure of heavenly merit.

A few street children actually worked. There were small

merchants in the area of the Gara who always needed help unloading merchandise and were willing to pay kids for temporary help. However, the money gained by this means was very little. There were also restaurants looking for kids to clean in front and carry out garbage in back. In those cases, payment was usually made in leftover food. A good worker, however, could endear himself to the owner of a business and eventually receive other help such as clothing.

There were those who sold newspapers. A professional vendor would entrust a stack of newspapers to a boy who would then choose a position in the Gara from which to sell. Often those who bought a paper would give the boy the change or a tip; in that way the boy would have a fair amount left over after paying the vendor.

Other boys stationed themselves around the parking areas and offered to wash cars. A variation was for a boy to carry a bottle of soapy water and a squeegee. He would stand at an intersection and, when cars stopped for a red light, work his way up the line washing windshields. When I did this I would always ask the driver if he wanted his windshield washed because many times after a windshield was washed, the driver would refuse to give anything on the grounds he hadn't requested the service.

Sometimes farmers would come into the city looking for street kids to work as shepherds or cowherds but they were paid very, very little. Of course the boy would receive food, but since they were used to being free or having more money or having drugs, the work didn't suit them.

Selling drugs is another method of business on the streets. These are not the hard drugs used in affluent countries, but a simple substance called "aurolac," a kind of lacquer sold in relatively small bottles. The majority of street children use aurolac. They pour a bit of it into a plastic bag, put the bag over their mouth and breathe it in. It does several things to and for them. One, it makes them drunk. Two, it takes away hunger pains. Three, it assuages their suffering from the cold. Four, it makes them forget their problems.

In the course of a week a boy will purchase several bottles of aurolac and then sell them on Saturday and Sundays when the stores are closed. A bottle sold on Sunday can bring a fivefold profit over the purchase price.

Many of us would rather spend our money buying aurolac than food. It was our refuge, our escape, our pacifier—that which allowed us to forget the reality of our situation. The drug also caused us to hallucinate. I saw things moving around in the sky. Others saw ships of extraterrestrials landing and discharging little men.

It also anesthetizes, so one doesn't feel pain. When we were on drugs and someone beat us, we didn't feel a thing. We were not exactly addicted in the way a person would be addicted to heroin, but we did come to depend on the drug.

I remember my first experience with aurolac. Another boy offered me a plastic bag containing a dose. I put the bag over my mouth and inhaled several times. First I saw stars. Then I passed out. When I awoke I had no idea of where I was, and when I looked about, to my chagrin, I was in the women's rest room.

Every one of us knew all the stores where aurolac was sold. We spent half of every day combing the city of Bucharest for our drug supply. Many, when they couldn't find a supply in Bucharest, went sixty kilometers to Ploiesti—fifty minutes by train. It was considered a major crisis when there was no aurolac to be found. Something like a shock wave went through the street kid community. Everyone followed everyone else around to discover if anyone had even a drop of aurolac. If anyone was found to have any, it was sure to be stolen. Those who were smart sold their aurolac before it was stolen. When there was a shortage, it brought a price six times higher than normal.

There was a man about sixty years old who dealt in aurolac continually. He always seemed to have it. There was a group of boys who were intermediaries between the old man and those searching for drugs. One time some big kids caught the old man alone with aurolac on him, and they beat him with a crowbar. He survived.

One day when I was unusually flush with money I bought sixteen bottles of aurolac—but not to sell. They lasted four days. I shared them, and we got high everywhere: in the garbage bins, on the streets, sidewalks and passageways in the Gara. We were not the least embarrassed at our condition. Society didn't like us, and we didn't like society. People looked at us, but they didn't say anything. Even the police took notice of us but said nothing.

Some kids carried their plastic bags of aurolac in a pocket, others inside their shirt, while others carried the bags in their hands. The bags often broke, leaving them stained with aluminum lacquer.

It goes without saying that many survive by stealing— big kids as well as little. They break into stores, kiosks, fruit stands and cars. Most of what they steal they sell unless it is something they can eat. Some street kids steal from other street kids. Big boys rob people on the streets at night. Their easiest marks are drunks who have passed out. The boys take their wallets, jackets, watches—whatever.

There is an endless variety, so of course there are the pickpockets. They watch for travelers who have a wallet so full it is conspicuous. Sometimes a gang will work together to distract a person while the most adept filches the billfold.

Then there are the pay phone specialists. They know how to dismantle an entire telephone in order to get the money out. However, in the past couple of years all coin phones have been replaced by card phones, thus putting the phone thieves out of business.

Yet another way of making money is to beg at stoplights. Kids go from car to car as they are waiting for the light to change, begging money for "bread." They choose especially busy intersections for their trade. As one may imagine, there is tremendous rivalry for positions at these stoplights, and some kids will show up at an especially early hour of the morning to secure their position.

Some of the street kids will try anything; one can't help but admire their cleverness. A boy I knew named Vali accosted an Orthodox priest one day.

"Father, may I ask you a question?"

"Of course, my son; what is it?"

"Well, Father, is it better to steal or to beg?"

The priest replied, "Why, of course it is much better to beg."

Vali smiled mischievously and said, "Then give me a dollar!"

The last category of street kid is involved in prostitution. There are many young children hired out to foreigners for sexual purposes, though also to Romanians. These children are under the control of a pimp who collects the money for his "merchandise." Many children are forced into this kind of life, though others enjoy it and engage in it willingly.

Of course, there are also girls used in this way. The pimps take much of the money they earn. Some girls are held virtual prisoners in houses where they are used continuously.

Sex is a way to make money and survive, but sex is a part of the life of any street child, whether or not they are involved in prostitution.

CHAPTER 9

The Role of Sex on the Streets

L iberty is the most precious possession of the street kids. The majority of them would renounce a family life if it were offered to them. They don't like rules, restrictions, limitations or responsibilities. They want total liberty. So they go about self-reliant and unconstrained—and this attitude extends into their sexual life.

This opens into a fuller discussion of the subject of the sexual life of the street child. I suppose some will find the topic unpalatable, but sex plays a major role in the children's lives—a kind of deviant pacifier for those denied natural affection.

The majority of the street kids, including the small ones, are sexually active—intensely so. Even many pre-pubescents have a well-developed sex life and know more about the subject than some adults. Their imaginations are advanced; their thoughts go off in all directions as to how to fulfill their sexual urges—anything from group sex to rape. They have been well instructed from all sides and, naturally, have picked up a lot from the mass media: the newspapers with their daily uninhibited fare of pornography, along with television and films. These have had an extraordinary influence on stimulating their impulses. So, for many of the street kids, sex is not only a pleasure but also a way of life.

Children, even though small, are taught everything about sexual relations. Take, for example, a girl of six or seven years of age. She comes into the Gara innocent, knowing nothing of the system or the risks. If she is pretty, at once she will be surrounded by a group of admirers, boys twelve or thirteen years old, and she will be drawn into their group. They will talk with her, joke with her and eat together. But afterwards they will invite her to the place where they sleep. There, with or without her approval, she will be forced to have sexual relations and thus lose her innocence.

This does not apply only to girls. Little boys will also be subjected to the same system against their will by those who prefer them.

Many boys have escaped from orphanages where they had already suffered abuse. They arrive on the streets used and experienced. The ones who, through seasoning, have become confirmed homosexuals are called "older brothers." These "older brothers" follow a new arrival and size him up: Is he a virgin? Is he handsome? They analyze his movements and behavior. If the new boy meets the qualifications of one of the older brothers, then the older brother sets out to conquer—to win him over. The older boy will offer his target candy and other gifts; he will even supply him with his own portion of food so as to keep him contented. Then the older boy announces to all that the younger boy is under the protection of his "older brother"; if anyone touches his ward, he will have to deal with him. Thus, between the younger boy and his homosexual protector a solid, powerful relationship develops in which the boy feels protected and befriended. Only after this preparation does the older boy begin to use the younger. Through the gifts, protection and friendship the groundwork has been laid to make the younger boy more receptive to the arrangement.

On the streets, a handsome, untouched boy, if he comes within sight of a homosexual, will be violated by force if he cannot be won by other means. The older boy makes preparations by sending his spies to find out where the younger boy sleeps, what areas he frequents and what possibilities he has for hiding so if the younger boy attempts to flee, he can be found.

Since many of the boys on the streets came from the orphanages, they were already confirmed in their sexual preferences before they hit the streets. Likewise, many older boys on the streets spent time in "schools of correction"—juvenile detention facilities. As mentioned, in many of these places, two boys are placed together to sleep because there are insufficient beds. This virtually guarantees corruption.

So, homosexuality propagates itself among the street children. A boy comes into the community of street children somewhat innocent, never having had relations with a girl or knowing much about sexual matters. He is introduced to sexual practices by another male, and, if he finds pleasure in such activity, it is fairly certain he will be captured the rest of his life.

In prostitution, whether male or female, the master over the prostitutes is a "peste" (fish), or a pimp. He is the one who negotiates with a customer concerning the "merchandise." These pimps collect the money and decide how much the boy or girl is to receive. A pimp can be a street person or someone else. Once a boy has been violated he is put out to work, and, in time, he begins to enjoy his trade.

The pimp is used to dealing with a wide variety of clients. Some are local; some come from foreign countries. Some want young boys; others are looking for strong boys in their mid-teens. It is the custom, however, for the pimp not to force little boys into prostitution unless it is their own idea.

Much of what is written about the boys applies also to girls. It is the same system. One might ask why a boy or girl would allow themselves to be used by the pimps. But, of course, living on the streets they lack money, food, protection—and some have mental problems. So they either approach the pimp themselves or are recruited by him to work. If the boy or girl has no experience, he or she will be taught the trade.

If a pimp ever has problems with one of his workers, such as resistance or running away, he will resolve the problem through fear. His methods can be terrifying and effective.

Up to this point I have presented sex as an occupation for street kids, but there is also another side.

Since street kids learn to survive at a tender age and are presented with life's problems much earlier and in greater intensity than an average person, in general their experience in handling problems is greater. Proportionally, their knowledge and experience in sexual matters also increase.

Most street kids are more developed or knowledgeable in regard to sexual matters than are their counterparts in the normal world.

When a child enters a clique of street kids, in time he or she will take on the characteristics and habits of that group. There are cliques that take a girl at night to where they stay, and all will use her with or without her permission.

Other cliques are harsh in their punishment of "traitors." Their leaders force sexual perversions on miscreants, and lessons are given with beatings.

Other cliques practice group masturbation. If anyone refuses, it means he has no part with that group. For street kids, masturbation is something normal. Their inspiration comes from the newspapers, which contain quite enough pornography to arouse even the most insensitive. When I say newspapers, by the way, I don't mean sleazy tabloids. I mean the major, legitimate national press, which could only be sold from under the table in a place like America because of its content. It is excused on the grounds of being an expression of the liberated European attitude. The most prestigious national daily even runs an information page now and then, divulging where prostitutes are available, what price and what services are offered.

For most kids, sexual relations are a matter of pride, and they boast of their practices and exploits. Their imaginations are ample, and they put into practice what they envision. Perversions extend into cross-dressing. Many, when they become bigger, abuse the younger children with the excuse that it was what was done to them.

I have been frank in presenting the faults and customs of

the street child in all their starkness. As already mentioned, some may be revolted. But one needs to see the entire picture before judging. In the Bible, the ninth chapter of John, a young man born blind is brought to Jesus. The question is asked, *Who sinned in the matter of this boy being born blind: he or his parents?* That is an entirely valid question regarding the street child. Who is at fault for his depraved existence? And like Job of old, the child cries out, "Have pity on me, my friends, have pity, for the hand of God has touched me" (Job 19:21)—only in the case of the street child, we might ascribe his condition more to the action of Satan than of God. And, like those who came to comfort Job, there are those who come to accuse while others console.

CHAPTER 10

A Place to Sleep

In October of 1992 I met two university students majoring in social service. After I explained my situation to them, they offered to put me in a hostel where I could get a bed and food. I accepted their offer. The hostel was called Pinocchio House and had been established as a refuge for street kids—but I had to wait two days to get in.

The weather turned cold that night, and it rained hard. I slept in the stairway of an apartment building. I didn't go to the Gara because I was afraid of being picked up by the police and losing my chance to go to Pinocchio. I wanted to see what kind of a place it was, and if it wasn't what I wanted, I would escape.

The day after, I met with the students again, and they registered me in Pinocchio House. I liked it there. No one beat me, and I had a bed, clothes and good food.

In time I made friends with the director, and she saw I was a boy who could be trusted. There was a teacher of music there who organized a choir, and when another center was inaugurated, we went there to sing. What I didn't know was that the whole thing was filmed and broadcast on national television. Some neighbors back in Buzau were amazed to see me on television and told my parents.

I learned to play chess at Pinocchio and began to think of getting back in school. In time I was appointed chief over a group of boys, and in that way I became the second most trusted boy among the seventy children in the center. I had good rapport with some of the staff, and they would give me spending money from time to time. That way I was able to buy cigarettes.

In March 1993, I succeeded in getting into school. I went daily with another trusted boy and passed in all my subjects.

I was happy and doing well, but then disaster struck: In April 1993 my mother came to take me home. I didn't want to go. I wanted to stay there, but legally they had to make me go with her if she insisted. Thus, I found myself back in Buzau.

On the way home, my mother told me my beloved grandmother had passed away. I was not at all happy to hear the news—in fact, I was crushed. My mother tried to comfort me by saying that in comparison with most seventy-three-year-old women, my grandmother had had an easy death. But I would like to have been there before she died and seen her one last time.

I returned to school and finished seventh grade, failing

only in a Romanian literature class, which I had to make up in a brief summer session. It was the last time I would see the inside of a school for another year and a half.

After finishing summer school I decided to go to work at the farm again. I only lasted a month. Someone stole a salami and put the blame on me, but I knew nothing about it.

Later, in August, my father, out of pure revenge over my lost wages he would have gained, took me with him to steal from the fields where I had worked. I went four nights in a row: one night with him and the other nights alone. We stole three sacks each of tomatoes and onions.

Although I tried to adjust to living with my family, I could not. My thoughts were still fixed on total liberty. Therefore, that same August I left home once again for Bucharest, where I intended to remain forever.

I was thirteen, and already it seemed like I should be an old man. At least I was an old hand at traveling. By now the route was so familiar I knew every mile of the way.

The first order of business upon arrival in Bucharest was to find my old gang. I waited around half a day to see if any of them would appear. Finally some of them started showing up. But much had changed in my absence. There were new boys in the gang, and some of the old ones were no longer around. Even the place they slept had changed. They were now sleeping in the attic of the Gara—though they also used the basement where the archives were stored.

Reaching the roof of the Gara was a challenge in itself. There was a stairway leading from the basement that wound up three more floors to some apartments built over the main leg of the Gara. At the second floor landing was a window that had to be opened. Standing on the sill, we had to chin ourselves up a meter to a ledge that led past the windows of the apartments. After negotiating a distance of six meters (twenty feet), we climbed up another meter onto the roof of the Gara. Once on the roof, there were a number of trapdoors by which we could enter the attic.

There was yet one more place I used to sleep, and that was the garbage bin in back of the Gara. It was in an area surrounded by a fence and right around the corner from a narrow, grassy area frequented day and night by street people of all ages: drunk and drugged. It was an area even the police avoided, so for me it was a haven.

When a child is on the street without a home, without food, without knowing anyone who can even give him a place to stay, it is difficult to survive when the sky is the only roof over his head.

When I arrived the first time on the streets I slept in the Gara in the winter and among the bushes in the summer. But there are many who sleep in the "canals," the tunnels under the streets that carry hot water pipes. They drag pieces of cardboard down there and use them for beds. Others sleep in the basements of apartment buildings, while still others make use of the stairways. Yet others sleep in the attic of the Gara, in empty rooms, in the waiting rooms, in garbage bins, in trains whether parked or moving, in subway stations and wherever else their ingenuity leads them.

There are some among them who bed down with Gypsy families and even beg for them in the daytime. When I was small and new to Bucharest, a Gypsy family took me into their house with the idea that I would beg for them, but when I wouldn't, they threw me out. There were other kids, however, who didn't mind the arrangement and would beg for the Gypsies. In return, they were given protection, food and a place to stay as long as they brought in money.

When street kids travel on the trains, the first item of business after the train pulls out is avoiding the conductor. After that they seek out an unoccupied compartment where they curl up on an empty row of seats and go to sleep. (A compartment contains two rows of opposing seats with room for six in first class and eight in second class.)

The largest cities have garages where trains are parked to be cleaned and inspected. Many children make use of the empty cars while they await attention.

Those who sleep in the depot waiting rooms stretch out on benches if there is room, or crawl up into baggage racks, while others simply curl up on the concrete floor. Whatever, they try to be a close as possible to a radiator for warmth. Where there is enough space, groups of children will curl up together in a ball and sleep through the night. Often the police come along, poke the kids awake with their nightsticks and evict them from their resting place. A half-hour later the kids are all back in place.

Some go out on the platforms where the trains depart and curl up on the waiting benches. It is, of course, very cold out there in the winter, but it is a place where the police rarely bother them.

Especially in the daytime, one can observe children sleeping in the subway trains.

I slept in a lot of such places. My favorite location was in the attic of the Gara. There wasn't enough room to stand upright, but it was a secure roof over my head. There were lots of places to choose from since the Gara was a large building—in fact, three structures joined together as one.

As mentioned, the basement of the Gara was the archive where all kinds of documents, registers and other papers were brought for storage. Many of us slept there. There was a large hot water pipe that passed through the area, and we climbed up on it for warmth while we slept. At first it was dark, but I noticed electric wires and finally figured out how to connect a bulb so we could have light.

Another place in which we slept was a garbage bin in back of the Gara. That was the best place to hide when we were running from the police. For me the smell, the pieces of broken glass, the cold—all became normal over time, and I was not the least ashamed to sleep on top of a heap of rotting garbage.

Often, when I had stayed out too late in central Bucharest I would just sleep in the stairwell of a convenient apartment building or in the basement. I met a lot of other kids in such places. In that same category were the buildings under construction. Hundreds were left unfinished after the Revolution, and although cold in winter, those places were secure from harassment.

One evening I chose the stairwell of an apartment building to sleep in, and I almost met my end. I had been to a theater where I met a girl and started conversing with her. She was a lot older than I—six or seven years older. I offered to walk her home, but on the way my emotions boiled over and I started kissing her. We got to her apartment and took the elevator to her floor. She gave signs that she was "willing," but something kept me from going into her apartment, and I left without doing anything.

Since it was too late to get back to the Gara, I chose a nearby apartment building and climbed up to the eleventh floor—the highest floor in Romanian apartments. The buildings are limited to eleven floors because the Romanian elevator industry does not make a lift that will go any higher. I fell asleep and somehow rolled over and fell down the stairwell. I was not aware of falling, and I must have been knocked unconscious, too, because I didn't know anything until morning when I awoke to find myself in a pool of blood and my forehead smashed. I left the building and began to ask passersby the way to the nearest hospital. At the hospital a doctor sewed me up and bandaged my wound.

The next day I went looking for the girl, but when I found her, she ignored me, and I let the matter drop.

I mentioned already the canals, the tunnels that carried hot water and utility pipes under the streets. There were two canals near the Gara where many children slept. It was one of the few areas the police were afraid to enter. All the big cities had these canals, and fugitive children could be found in all of them.

The last category was composed of children who slept in the bushes and shrubbery. This was possible only in the summer because it was warm. But it was never pleasant. One was attacked by hordes of mosquitoes and had to find a place well hidden enough so as not to be bothered by anyone.

One time when I was twelve, I was sleeping in the bushes in one of the parks. I started out alone, but later some other kids came along and settled down in the same bushes. They had with them a tarpaulin made for a car, which we used as a blanket. When we were fast asleep, a squad of police with flashlights and two dogs came along and found us there. They woke us up and put handcuffs on us. The problem was that in that same night someone had broken into one of the major stores in Bucharest. They picked me to arrest because my footprints matched those left at the scene of the crime, and they arrested the others because they were carrying the tarp. At the precinct station they locked us in a cell after taking all the identity information and fingerprinting us. What really upset me was that I had just run away from home that morning, and already I was arrested.

In the end, they discovered I was innocent of the crime they were investigating and eventually let me go, but not before they forced me to make some false declarations about breaking into telephones. I didn't think too much about it and just wanted to get out of there, so I didn't refuse. In spite of cooperating with the police, it took me five days to get out. During the entire five days I was incarcerated I ate only once, and that was because of the kindness of someone who came to visit another prisoner.

CHAPTER 11

Bored
and High

Becuase I had been gone from the Gara almost a
year, it took me a while to get back into the gang.
A change from the past was that the gang contained a couple who were expecting a child. I don't know
where she was coming from, but he was a country boy. At
this time my gang had a friend, also named Catalin. He
was an athlete and belonged to a club. Many times when
we had trouble with other gangs stronger than us, he
defended us. He had a dog, and he would take the dog's
chain and whip others that threatened us. He had a small
business near the Gara selling fruit, so we helped him any
way we could by carrying his merchandise. He lived in one
of the apartments over the Gara, so he gave us access to
both the attic and the basement.

As soon as I got back in the gang, I started in with the
aurolac again. I went out in the morning begging and

would continue until around 3:00 o'clock in the afternoon. But with most all the money I gained from begging, I would buy aurolac. After I got back to the Gara in the late afternoon the "party" would begin, and I would stay high until midnight.

There was a time when all I did was seek drugs and stay high. I was in rebellion against the world. I had my own world. I was torn up inside, but I didn't want to do anything about it.

In the evenings when we didn't have light in the basement or the attic, I would go to an Orthodox church and steal candles.

One time I entered a church and sat down to observe. I had not the least idea of what they did in such a place, but I felt quiet inside, so I stayed a while in an attitude of respect coupled with fear. I observed the conduct of others in the church. Some were silent. Others had their heads bowed, and some were crying while others seemed sad. I was struck by the fact that no one in that place was happy. Then a priest came and started doing "magical" things. I was mystified as to what it was all about. He began to address the crowd in Romanian, but I couldn't understand a thing he was saying. As for what was going on in that place, it was as if I had ears, but couldn't hear; eyes, but couldn't see.

Due to the fact that it was warm in the church and my lice had awakened and started eating on me, I got up and left. I was embarrassed to scratch myself while inside such an apparently serious place.

I should explain about the parasites to which we were

host. Living in the streets we were exposed to all types of insects such as fleas, lice and the itch mite. We were especially loaded with lice. We had lice that lived on our skin and lice that lived in our clothing. I had a friend who spent considerable time every morning trying to kill all the lice he found crawling on him. Needless to say, he never succeeded.

There were only a couple places set up to help us street kids. One of them, a humanistic Catholic organization called Caritas, opened an office in the Gara around December 1993 with a feeding station and a few beds where smaller kids could sleep at night. Every morning from 8:00 to 9:00 and every noon from 12:00 to 1:00 meals were served, and many of the street kids took advantage of it. Often there was a line of fifty kids waiting to get in. Caritas also distributed clothing, but often the bigger boys made off with the best clothing before the little ones got any.

There was an American named John who distributed sandwiches in the evening when Caritas was closed. He had some men working for him who made and dispensed the sandwiches—and they were very good sandwiches. I did not meet him at that time, nor did I even know his name, but I did enjoy the sandwiches.

In that way, we had access to food three times a day. For me personally, because I had access to food, clothing, cigarettes, drugs and a place to sleep, I thought of the Gara as my home.

When one puts together all the activities of the street children—begging, singing on trains, searching through garbage, stealing, watching films and exploring—it would seem that their time is quite occupied. In reality, most of their time is spent in idleness. When the Gara was open to them, small groups of children would simply circulate through the building from one end to the other, down into the subway station, back around and up into the Gara again. Going slowly, a circuit could occupy as much as thirty minutes. After a couple of circuits they would find a place over to the side where they could just sit and do nothing. In the winter it was uncomfortable: The cement floor was cold and the Gara was cold. The building was entirely open at the train platforms, and there was no possibility of heating anything other than the waiting rooms. Whatever cold the children felt, however, was mitigated by their ubiquitous bag of aurolac.

CHAPTER 12

Crazy

In those days I realized life made no sense to me. I no longer wanted to talk to anyone about my family or about my little sister and my brothers—nothing about my personal identity. So in September 1993 when I turned fourteen I decided to change my name. No longer would I be Catalin Dobrisan, but henceforth I would be known as "Nebunica." It's hard to translate that exactly into English. *Nebun* means "crazy," and the *ica* made it into a name. I made it clear to everyone, "Don't call me Catalin anymore. I am now Nebunica."

I decided to forget the reality around me. I wanted to lose my identity. I didn't want anyone to know any longer who I was or where I was.

I consumed a lot of aurolac. I was dizzy and befuddled most of the time. I started drinking, too: beer, wine—anything I could get. Then something happened to put a stop at least to the drinking. I was hanging around with an older street person near the Hotel Dorobanti, near the Plaza Romana, and one evening I started partying with him,

drinking vodka and wine. Before long, I was dead drunk—
so drunk I had no idea even what time it was. I dimly
understood I needed to get back to the Gara, so I set out
on foot toward University Plaza. By that time I could no
longer stand upright, so I went along on all fours like a dog.
So dizzy I thought I would pass out, I entered an apartment building and somehow climbed up to the second
floor landing where I fell asleep. I was awakened the next
morning by a woman screaming at me that she was going
to call the police.

After I fled that place I did some thinking. I decided
then and there that I would never again imbibe.
Considering my lifestyle, it is unusual that I stuck by that
decision and never drank liquor again.

The more time passed, the more my life plunged into a
state of disaster. All around me were nothing but people
who were drugged, homosexuals, rapists, prostitutes,
drunks, brawlers—all coupled with sadness and loneliness.

A street child has a low self-image, he has self-hatred,
and he is in despair—and he has many other traits that go
with being a street child. One of the outward manifesta-
tions of these internal negative attitudes is self-mutilation.
They cut diagonal lines an inch to an inch and a half long
across the top of their forearms. If done with a razor blade,
the scar will be thin. But those who use a piece of broken
glass will leave a scar as much as three-eighths of an inch
wide. A few will also cut their neck, stomach and chest.

Why would anyone do such a gruesome thing? There
are several reasons. One, it shows fortitude and toughness
in front of the other kids. Even girls cut themselves for

that reason. Others do it out of frustration; they are upset about something or even begin to miss their families. Such an act surely takes their mind off their mental pain. Of course, when high on aurolac, they feel very little of the pain associated with the cutting.

Perhaps the deed has a more mystical meaning going back to ancient times, associated with dark powers that even the children are not aware of. We read in the Bible that the prophets of Baal cut themselves until the blood flowed.

Some kids keep a blade on them at all times. If arrested by the police, they will pull out the blade and start cutting. There is very little any kid can do to impress a policeman, but this is one of them. It is the one thing the police view with revulsion. Perhaps the only thing that would gain a child his freedom faster would be to start vomiting all over the place. To the police, the public and even other street kids, this one act projects an image of mental illness. Though I wanted others to think I was crazy, this was one of the things I did not do.

When the holiday season came, I sang Christmas carols on the subway trains once again. I made money that way, and I could say life picked up a bit except that I spent almost everything on aurolac and cigarettes. Caritas gave out clothing, so I looked a bit better. Nevertheless, while the rest of the populace was celebrating the season, it didn't seem like any kind of holiday to me since I considered I had no family. I thought about my family, but I knew I could never go back to them. So I passed Christmas begging and singing in the trains.

It was winter and cold, but soon I no longer had a jacket.

A street kid's wardrobe is probably the only thing about him that continually changes. An aid worker came to the Gara one evening with a half dozen beautiful new sweatshirts to give to the street kids. He chose the recipients carefully. Within thirty minutes the sweatshirts could be seen on young college students blocks away from the Gara. The money gained from the sales was used for aurolac.

After New Year's I lost all ambition for a while to go into the city, so I stayed close to the Gara. I would ride the subway trains and beg, but since the trains departed from the Gara and returned there, it was as if I had never actually left the Gara at all. Again, most of the money was wasted on imprudence. I continued eating from the garbage bins and whatever leftovers I could find.

Since I now carried the name of "Crazy," I intended to act like it. When it was warm outside I dressed for winter: a couple of sweaters and a greatcoat. It looked weird, but, of course, I was crazy. I walked up and down the twelve train platforms with an empty two-liter soda bottle under my left arm and a broomstick in my right hand, looking for scraps to eat in the garbage barrels. If I found something, I would either put it in my pocket or eat it on the spot. There was no logic as to why I carried the bottle and the broomstick. I was crazy. I'm sure people thought, *There goes one of those wretched street kids.*

So things had become worse for me. I wanted freedom, but I had become a slave of poverty, privation, vagrancy, misery—of nothingness. In my rejection of sanity, I was in the early stages of complete personality disintegration. If allowed to continue it would come to fruition, probably producing a state of permanent mental unbalance. Fortunately, enough diversions came my way to soon distract me from my trek toward madness.

CHAPTER 13

The Need to Steal

Sometimes I would try to separate myself from the Gara. At those times I would spend more time singing in the subway trains or hunched down in a seat at the cinema watching whatever film came along. But even if I hung around central Bucharest there were always street kids my age that I would fall in with. Although I usually got along with anyone, the other street kids were not friendly in every case. One incident that sticks in my mind occurred in winter. This time I was in my home territory in the park across from the Gara de Nord, and I saw a group of youths smoking. When I asked one of them for a light, they threw me to the ground, kicked me in the face and left me bleeding.

One evening when I was with a group of boys and we were a little drunk, I saw a kiosk. (This was before I swore off the booze.) There was liquor displayed in the window, but the place was closed. I picked up a stone, smashed the window and took a bottle of cherry liquor. We drank a bit and then settled down for the night in the basement of a nearby apartment building where there were some hot water pipes. In the morning, the watchman threw us out of there, but on the way out I noticed the bottle had disappeared. We tried to go back to the same place the next night, but we found everything locked up.

In those days, toward the end of 1993, I was involved several times in thefts with a boy who was called "The Chinaman" because of his Asian features. He was well known among the street kids for his penchant for breaking and entering. Most everyone considered him crazy. He was also well known to the police. In fact, on his identity document there was a red line, which meant mentally ill. All mentally ill persons carried identity documents with a red line.

One evening he invited me to go with him on a job. He had cased out a stand in the Plaza of the Aviators that sold cigarettes, newspapers, magazines, books, coffee and so forth. The breaking in was fairly simple. He had a crowbar with him that easily popped the padlock. He wanted me to be the lookout so he could do his "work" without having to be alert as to who might be coming.

I went with him several times. First we looked for a place, such as a construction site, to lay low most of the night. About 4:00 A.M. we went out and broke into our objective. I was always the lookout. One evening we found a whole box full of coins, which could be spent, but mostly we just took stuff.

Another time we set out with a crowbar and two sacks to do a job. We were looking for an apartment building to sleep in when the police stopped us. They asked for our identity papers, which we didn't have. Coupled with the fact we were carrying two sacks, it made us look pretty suspicious, so the police hauled us into the precinct station. They wrote down basic information and then separated the two of us. At that point I decided to come clean and tell the truth. I told the police what we were up to and made a written declaration. They kept us there two days and then let us go. What worked out in our favor was that we were not carrying the crowbar when arrested. That was my last adventure with "The Chinaman." I told him I would rather beg than steal. Besides that, he never divided the spoils fairly. I got very little out of our escapades considering the risk.

Although I was not above stealing what I needed, my custom was more to beg, sing on the trains or go through the garbage. Some kids stole exclusively. When one thinks about it, one rat will not consume much grain, but in countries such as India, the total rat population together devours a huge percentage of the harvest—food that is needed by the masses. In the same way, one street kid does not steal that much, but when one puts the total together and calculates the amount that each must steal in a day to survive, it adds up to a tremendous loss to the economy.

A Belgian organization that was trying to help us put me on a list of kids they were taking to the Carpathian Mountains on an excursion. So, in January 1994, forty of us kids headed out of Bucharest on the train for two weeks of fun in the snow. When we arrived, cabins had been rented for our quarters. I stayed only a week. Even though those responsible for the trip tried hard and spent a lot of money to show us deprived kids something different and tried to be friends with us, they did not really succeed. I heard later that at the end of the trip the kids embarked on a rampage of destruction, and the excursion ended in failure.

The same organization also attempted to work with street kids during the day, especially teaching them a trade such as carpentry—or some activity. Among the latter, they put together a circus. There was a Frenchman who trained some of us in acrobatics and other circus arts. In that way, I learned to juggle. In 1994 they formed a circus troupe in which I was engaged as a juggling clown. We put on a show in Bucharest and afterwards were interviewed on the radio. I asked to say something and was handed the mike, but I spent the whole time talking against my father and what he had done to me. I said I hoped he would see now that I had changed and was going to make something of myself. But after that one performance, I left the group. The others continued putting on performances in other locations.

CHAPTER 14

My Uncle
and the Cows

Winter was severe. My shoes were ripped and had holes in the soles; I had no hat, no gloves, no jacket. The Belgian organization convinced me that I should return home. They gave me some new clothes and some money. I was afraid to go home, however, so I decided to go to my Uncle Dumitru's. It was March 1994. I realized I had no life in the Gara. I wanted to live. I wanted to marry and have my own family with my own children near me, but I had no hope of any of it.

Nevertheless, I was now on a train headed for my uncle's with the hope that I would find, in that locality where I had grown up, something that would change my life. I was definitely searching, but I only vaguely knew for what.

I arrived at my uncle's country home. I was surprised to learn that his wife had passed away. He was now a widower and his family disintegrated. Of his two children, one was adopted and another in an orphanage. He was a very lazy man—not working at any kind of a regular job. As a result, he was poverty stricken. The only food he had on hand was cornmeal for cornmeal mush, onions and, now and then, sheep cheese.

In the daytime he would occasionally go work with a group in the fields. Some, witnessing his situation, took pity on him and offered him the job of village cowherd. The total number of cows owned by the villagers was five hundred. Having no other means of support, my uncle accepted the offer.

This was about the time I arrived, so I agreed to help him. First of all we realized five hundred were too many cows to care for, so another man was hired. He took half, and we took the other half. Our pay was to be both in cash and produce.

Our two hundred fifty cows were owned by seventy-five families. Three families a week had to give us produce, so, once a week, my uncle sent me to collect the vegetables due us, and he went to collect the money. Finally my uncle was earning something.

Uncle Dumitru headed out early in the morning to tend the cows. After I milked our own cow, I led it out to join the rest. I stayed with my uncle the whole day the first two months. It was hard work because I had to run a lot, and often I was barefoot or in torn sneakers.

We began to eat a bit better and to have enough. At 4:00 o'clock every afternoon I got free of the cows for a while and came home to cook supper. (The neighbors taught me how to cook.) After the food was ready I went to bring our cow home. I worked hard and had a lot of responsibility.

Each village family owned about seven acres of land. The system was not like in America where farmers own large tracts upon which they can grow a surplus and make a profit. In rural Romania each family expected to grow just enough to support itself. Of course, if they did have a surplus, it could be taken and sold in the marketplaces in the larger cities. They also sold pigs, sheep, milk and extra eggs. But their major means of living came from their own plot of land, and what excess they had went to providing things they could not grow or make for themselves. They either succeeded in producing a good harvest, or they starved. By this system they were not used to having or needing a lot of cash. I remember a man came from the city wanting to buy a farm and had no success. The peasants said, "But if we sold to you, what would we do with the money?"

In addition to the seven acres, each family had a home garden. Villages were not laid out in squares as in the West but in a single, long street with houses on either side. Usually the house was adjoined by a wall across the front at the street. The lots are about fifty feet wide and five hundred or more feet long. That long, narrow plot contained the home garden, pig pen, chicken coop and shed.

In many villages the larger acreage was combined together to form a cooperative under the control of a farming association. Instead of each family growing ten major kinds of crops on its acreage, the sum total of all land was divided into ten parcels, and a major crop grown on each parcel. It sounds like another form of Communism, but it was not. Actually, it worked pretty well.

Summer came, and my uncle sent me to the association to find out where we would have land—what parcels we were to farm. I received five acres of corn and sunflowers, which I was expected to keep cultivated and weeded. When the corn began to grow I had to get out there and hoe in the summer heat. There was a little land left over, and I planted a vineyard on it.

My uncle gave me a lot of freedom. The only problem with my uncle was that he was a sot—a big one. Every evening, after finishing work, he would start drinking. Because of this he was deeply in debt, and everything he earned went to pay off his debts. Everyone in the area had vineyards, and there was a lot of wine to be had. So all my help did not really advance him a bit.

In time, my mother heard I was there and came to see me several times. She would stay two or three days and then try to convince me to return home, but I made it clear I never wanted to go back.

After working hard six months I realized my uncle was not the least thankful for all the work I had done and the help I was to him. I was on another dead-end road, and I decided it was time to move on. I came with nothing and left with nothing. I didn't even have a bag to carry with me when I left. People asked me, "Where are you going, Catalin?"

"Back to where I came from," I answered.

I went to Buzau, contacted my mother and told her I was going back to Bucharest. She didn't know what to say. She was very sad. She met me in town and went with me to the train. As I was getting on the train she said, "I hope that someday you, too, will spend sleepless nights wondering

where your child is, what he is eating, where he is sleeping."
Then she added, "I put you in the hands of God!" It
sounded good, but in reality she was angry and meant it as
a curse.

CHAPTER 15

Two Whole Chickens and a Prayer

T hus, in August 1994 I arrived back at the Gara. I was fourteen years old. Some people and organizations were now trying to help the street kids. I mentioned the American, who had a group of ten kids he was helping, but I didn't know anything about him except that he was sponsoring a feeding program every night in the Gara. He had a worker or two who made sandwiches and distributed them.

Now that I was back in the Gara I made myself a special daily schedule. I decided to use drugs less and less with the intention of quitting altogether. However, I continued begging at the stoplights, at the restaurants and the theaters. I planned a daily agenda that would take me to the Gara only at night. Things went better that way. I was not drugged so much and was able to think more clearly. I kept this pattern going for the next five months. Probably because of this I began to get tired of living in the streets and began to think more about the future. There wasn't a day I didn't think about what I would do if I could get more money—what would I do with it?

Having accustomed myself to begging at stoplights, I chose an intersection near a pizzeria. I went there almost every day. Upon arrival, the first item of business was to search through two large garbage bins behind the pizzeria. When I found a discarded piece of pizza, I was overjoyed and gobbled it down as fast as I could.

When I was finished with all the scraps of food I could find, I headed at once for the intersection where I began begging. I stayed no later than 11:00 P.M. so as not to miss the last streetcar to the Gara. I considered the Gara my home and had no desire to spend a night in any other part of the city.

Near the same intersection where I begged was a rotisserie where they sold baked chicken and potatoes by the kilogram. Sometimes I would station myself outside that establishment in the hope of picking up some change. Often I failed to get a single coin, but, to my surprise, I did get some of the chicken and garlic sauce. It was excellent. Once that happened, I set out as early as possible every morning to search through the garbage in back of the rotisserie in the hope of finding more chicken and bread. It was an exercise in patience.

My main stakeout at the rotisserie, however, was between 7:00 and 11:00 in the evening. I went every evening and

hung around begging unless the owner was there. That rotisserie did a big business in takeouts. Taxi drivers, rich people,
all kinds of people would stop there and buy prepared
chicken with garlic sauce, French fries and bread.

One autumn day in 1994 I had an especially beautiful
day. Someone gave me two whole baked chickens. For once
I didn't have to eat leftovers or garbage. I felt real gratitude
toward the man who so generously gave me the chickens.

I hesitate to deprecate in any way those who, by their
response to my begging, kept me alive so many years.
Begging plays a major part in the survival of the street kid,
so I don't think these insights into my life and the lives of
my derelict comrades would be complete without men-
tioning the motives of most who gave. It is not as in the
West where people give from motives of compassion.
There were few from the West who were not moved to
pity by the plight of the street kids. But the citizens of my
country tended to view the street child with more of a feeling of revulsion. They were the pariahs of society, and one
must keep one's distance from untouchables. Even those
from the West who came to help us were viewed with real
suspicion. What possible motive could they have for helping street kids except something sinister?

One of the wonders of Romania was that the majority
of its ordinary citizens managed to pass through forty-five
years of Communism with their Orthodox faith fairly
intact. Yet, their faith is built not so much upon a knowledge of their belief system, but upon a fear and reverence
for God that, at its core, is self-directed. Of course, not
only the Orthodox have this problem—perhaps the bulk

of Christendom is oriented thusly—but I mention them because the majority of the citizenry is Orthodox. So a coin is given to a street child not so much out of pity as out of expectation of some reward. In Spanish-speaking countries this principle is well understood, and beggars are quite straightforward about it—for they always say to their benefactors, "God will repay you!"

Whatever the motive, it did not diminish the benefit to us, and I was ecstatic over two whole chickens just placed into my hands. I had a bit of spare change from begging, so I bought a kilo of French fries and took all this to the basement room of the Gara where I found everyone drugged. At the same time, another guy arrived with some food, and we announced, "Dinner!" The others, sprawled around the room and seated on the floor against the walls, roused themselves out of their drug-induced stupor and tried to focus. One by one, they arose and stumbled over to where the food was set out. We gathered together around the repast, and everyone began to eat—except me. I stopped the others and called out, "Come on. Let's pray!" They all looked at me, shocked. Yes, I was crazy after all, but no one said anything because I had brought in the most food. I closed my eyes and began to pray. "I thank You, Lord, for this food which You have given us." I stopped for a moment, not used to praying and not knowing exactly what to say, and then continued, "And Lord, if You really exist, I ask You to take me out of this place. I am fed up with the lice, the dirt, eating garbage and sleeping in the trash bin. Give me a home to live in where I can grow up to be a normal person." I made the sign of the cross and began to eat. As I remember, it did not seem to be my conscious self praying, but rather my spirit crying to God for help.

Someone had given me a New Testament, and now I began to read it over and over, even though I didn't understand a thing. Nevertheless, I had a respect for The Book and was afraid of losing it.

One of the last persons one would ever expect to find in downtown Bucharest interacting with street kids was a sheep-herding peasant. These powerfully built men were wrapped from the neck to the ground in giant coats made of sheepskins with the natural fleece turned out. From a distance, one envisaged an encounter with an abominable snowman. They carried great, wooden staffs. The kids were generally afraid of them because they were uncaring and cruel. They took no gaff from anyone and would just as soon knock you down as look at you. The reason they came into the city was that they needed young shepherds. Village kids would not work for them because they offered so little pay—usually about two or three dollars a month to herd a flock of a hundred sheep. And woe betide the young shepherd who lost one. Even at that, many kids would go for awhile because they also received food.

Once one of those peasants hired me. After we had our agreement I told him I had to go get one more thing to take with me—and that was my New Testament. I worked for him only a week, but when I left I still had the New Testament. I also had one of those magazines the Jehovah's Witnesses hand out on street corners, and I read the whole thing. It was all about Gorbachev, Bush and the Pope.

There was another shepherd—an old man—and I started discussing what I read with him. He looked at me with wonder, thinking how smart I must be because he didn't understand a thing I was saying.

CHAPTER 16

Fifteen Years Old and Tired of Life

As another Christmas drew near, various groups singing Christmas carols began to show up in the Gara. I supposed some of them were Christians. I always stopped to listen to them. In fact, something came over me, and I was glued to the spot—as if I couldn't leave. Listening to them and seeing the way they were dressed and the happy expressions on their faces I thought, *Will I ever be that way?*

So the holidays came, and I sang once again in the subway. Most of the kids sang in a boy soprano, but I can't remember ever singing anything but bass. I seemed to collect a lot of money that year, but instead of buying drugs as I had in the past, I bought food. I continued going to the movies because I wanted to pretend I was a normal member of society just going out for the evening. When it was over I would go home. Unfortunately, when the film

109

ended, reality began, for the theatergoers all went to their respective domiciles, but I was still a vagrant.

That Christmas I got some new clothes from the Caritas organization. I felt different in the new clothes, but I wasn't happy. I was realizing that the kind of life I was living was too hard for me. One of the other boys in the Gara had put it this way: "I have no birthdays, no Christmas, no holidays, no life—it has all passed me by. In the winter I sleep in the subways; in the summer, outdoors. There is no meaning to it, and I cannot escape." However, when one begins to think this way, he is closer to escape than he realizes. It is those who don't realize it that are in trouble.

One evening I came back to the Gara and climbed up on the roof. There was a place on the edge where I went and cried. I meditated a long time on my life. Then I began to ask God, "Will I ever get out of this Gara? Will I ever have my own family—a wife and children? Will I ever have a profession?"

Another evening soon afterward, I was back up there again on the edge of the roof. It was the same day an elderly derelict had frozen to death. *I wonder if I will end up that way?* I thought. *Does my life have any value? Does anyone know I exist?* Thoughts of suicide began to pass through my mind. Life had had no meaning for me, and I had no hope it ever would, but I didn't have the courage to throw myself down. I reviewed my whole life. I saw everything I had done and realized I had hit bottom. I was in despair. I was fifteen years old and tired of the life of a street kid. I was fed up with my whole existence and my struggles—struggles that were directed only at survival.

After I prayed that God would release me from the Gara, things began to deteriorate rather than get better. Existence had become pretty much routine up to then, but now disturbing incidents began to intrude on the flow and rhythm of street life. With our low tolerance for frustration and the harshness of our lives, the only thing that made it bearable was a tranquil routine. Drugged much of the time, we could not adapt to disturbances in "the field."

Nelu, one of the boys in our gang, had foolishly assaulted another boy. With revenge in mind, the other boy got five others to join him in an attack on our gang. It happened to be a day when I had a lot of money on me and didn't need to go out to beg, so I was in the basement along with the rest when the other gang showed up. After beating Nelu to a pulp they left. I was guarding the knife we used to cut bread, and Nelu, in a rage, asked for it. He was drugged enough that he could not exercise restraint, so, afraid of what he would do, I refused to give it to him.

Thus, things were getting dangerous. I didn't realize it at the time, but incidents such as this were signs of impending release from my bondage.

Then something of great significance occurred. On the fifth of January 1995 I met in person the American I had only heard about who was helping the ten kids. Some called him "John," but most called him "Daddy." I was told he had come to Bucharest from Transylvania by pre-arrangement to pick up a boy from the Gara and take him to his home.

CHAPTER 17

Daddy

Since he played such a prominent part in my life, I must pause here to tell something about the man named John but who I and the kids call Daddy.

John had had a born-again experience at age twenty-two in 1954, more than twenty years before the term became popular. "I had been a very self-centered person," he recounts, "and spending my life serving the poor was the last thing I expected to do. An aptitude test in high school gave me an absolute zero in social work."

John had been trained as an electronics technician in the military, and after discharge, he headed to college. He had no intention of working with children—no interest in them—but after his freshman year, with nothing to do for the summer, he signed on as a counselor in a boys' camp. He was surprised to find that he got along well with the kids and had a knack for explaining difficult concepts in a way that could be easily understood. That led to choosing education as his major so he could become a teacher.

After graduation he joined the staff of a children's home

near New York City. Then, in 1961, he joined the faculty of the Christian Academy in Japan as a science teacher. The academy, CAJ, was a school near Tokyo established for the children of the English-speaking business and missionary community. Teaching was great, but John felt he wanted to be more directly involved with the care of children in difficulty.

He married Deana, a young woman with the same goals as his, in 1965. John quit teaching, and they began to work with some of the older mixed-blood boys—Japanese-Americans whose fathers had been members of the occupation forces. Three children were born to them in Japan.

In 1969 they headed to the States for a year of recuperation and fund-raising. Instead of returning to Japan, they got caught up in the youth revolution of that time. In 1970 they began working with hippies, transients, drug addicts and runaway kids in the southwestern state of New Mexico. In 1971 they established a facility in downtown Albuquerque that gave shelter and guidance to ten thousand young people over the next four years.

In late 1975 John went to Honduras, Central America to check out reports of children living in the streets. While there he opened a facility that began with twenty street children. Deana and their three children joined him, and they worked in Honduras the next seventeen years. John built six buildings, including a school for the children of the neighborhood poor and a beautiful chapel that drew much comment. In 1992 John turned over the entire project to a native church and returned to the United States. Their own three children were now adults, as were two Honduran boys they adopted who had become American citizens.

After returning to the United States, John and Deana discussed what they should do. John was now sixty, and he seriously considered retiring to work on his hobby, the music of Bach. But two weeks after arriving in the States, John had a dream that changed everything.

The dream was vivid. "I can still see it years later," he says. "I was standing on a sidewalk in a large city. In the dream I knew the city was Bucharest, Romania. It was all the more amazing because I had never been to Europe in my life. I was surrounded by a crowd of children about eleven to fourteen years of age. They were dirty, their clothes ragged and torn, and some had sores on their faces. They were talking excitedly to me in Romanian, but I had never heard the language and couldn't understand a word. When they realized I was not understanding them, they all gathered around me in a circle and held out their arms to me— and I knew they were asking me to come and help them."

Four months later John was on a plane headed to Romania. He was ready to go there knowing no one, but at the last minute he was put in touch with a businessman who agreed to meet his plane and show him around. When he left Romania two weeks later, he had a project open, five boys taken off the streets, a staff of four, the friendship of one of the mayors of Bucharest, and a document showing he was an honorary member of the prestigious Omenia Society. He says, "I couldn't believe it had all happened."

The businessman took John, along with fifty sandwiches,

to the Gara de Nord where he met his first crowd of street children. A nineteen-year-old boy who looked like a thug came up to him. John had been studying Romanian in the meantime and understood when the young man asked, "You know Jesus Christ?"

John replied, "Yes," and the boy shook his hand. That was Marius, who had been in prison eighteen months. Dumped out at the Gara with nowhere else to go and no future, Marius was in such despair that he vowed, "I will give it six months more, and if my situation doesn't change by then, I will kill myself." Marius is still with John to this day and is now a pastor.

A day or so after that first encounter, Marius and another nineteen-year-old met with John. The boys seemed angry about something, and John asked his businessman friend what they were saying. "They are saying that you are not the first one to show up here with a camera taking their pictures. Others have come, and they stayed in the fanciest hotel and ate in the best restaurants; they promised to come back, but they were never seen again. Maybe you are like them?"

John looked at the boys intently. "What I promise, I will do. I will stay where you stay and eat what you eat. If you sleep on the floor, I will sleep on the floor. But I will not abandon you." That was a major turning point. John had just committed himself to Romania and the children he saw in the dream.

John then searched for other adults working in the Gara with the children, but he was surprised to find no one. "Can I be the only one here?" he asked. The children nodded,

"Yes, you are the only one here in the Gara." It would be a
year or two before the others showed up.

On the plane back to the States John sat next to a
Romanian woman living in Canada. He told her all about
his experiences and plans. She looked at him and stated
matter-of-factly, "You're going to get hurt!" He had no
idea how badly, but he said later that even if he had known
the afflictions ahead, he would not have backed out.

On his next trip in March 1993 the number under care
was increased to ten, and the entire project moved from
Bucharest to the clean, quiet, Transylvanian city of Targu
Mures.

Transylvania is a historic part of northwestern
Romania. It is bounded on the west by Hungary, on the
north by Ukraine and on the east and south by the exqui-
site Carpathian Mountains. Politically, Transylvania was a
part of Hungary until ceded to Romania in 1918.

Romania had its origins in Transylvania when the
Romans entered the area occupied by the Dacian people
in A.D. 102 and set up a city called Napoca, now known
as Cluj-Napoca. The Roman emperor Hadrian visited the
area. The Romans had a great influence in Dacia. The
Roman soldiers intermarried with the local girls and gave
their name to both the country and the language, which is
based on Latin. Romania is, thus, unique: a Latin country
surrounded on all sides by Slavic people, except for the
northwest where it touches Hungary, a nation with its
own distinctive language, customs and people going back
to Attila the Hun.

Transylvania is also famous for its legendary character

Dracula, supposedly invented by an English author but, in reality, having his origin in a powerful Romanian ruler named Vlad Tsepes who lived in the fifteenth century. Vlad Tsepes was a notable patriot, but he was exceptionally cruel to his enemies, the Turks, whom he impaled on stakes. The name *Dracula* was then invented. In Romanian, *drac* means "devil." "*Dracul*" means "the devil." The letter a is added to make it a name.

The Transylvanian countryside consists mostly of high, rolling hills with broad valleys given over to agriculture. The Carpathian Mountains contain forest preserves, as do some of the higher hills.

In the year 1180, the Hungarian rulers of Transylvania, faced with an invasion by the Turks, called upon the Germans to immigrate and strengthen the defense of the area. Some say the mass migration of Germans from Germany to Transylvania gave rise to the legend of the Pied Piper of Hamlin.

The Germans built seven large cities called the "Siebenburgen" and dozens of smaller cities; they filled the valleys with agricultural villages. Large churches were constructed that impress tourists to this day. Even the small village churches were outfitted with pipe organs.

Of course, all the churches were Roman Catholic, but at the time of the Reformation, the archbishop of Transylvania journeyed to Germany and spent some time in consultation with Martin Luther. When the archbishop returned to Romania, he turned every last church from Catholic to Lutheran—and so they remain until this day. John was asked to be substitute organist at a large church in the ancient city of Sighisoara with its medieval architecture and atmosphere. The church was built in A.D. 1260. A plaque set in the wall of the stairway leading to the choir loft reads, "Renovated in 1484." The date carved into the ornate woodwork of the pipe organ reads, "1680." There is much history in the church. A marble plaque at the back lists the name of every pastor from the founding year of 1260 until the present.

At the front of the church is another marble plaque dedicated to the memory of those who died during World War II in defense of the "Fatherland." The Fatherland, of course, was Hitler's Germany, not Romania. The ethnic Germans paid a great price for siding with Hitler. In 1945, after the war, the Russians swept through Romania, rounded up all Germans between the ages of fifteen and fifty-five, and took them to Russia where they were used for five years in slave labor. In Romania, none but the very young and the very old were left. Then the Romanians surged through the German villages like gleaners and made off with farm equipment and animals, leaving the elderly and their young charges destitute.

After completing five years of slave labor in Russia, the German populace faced another forty years of Communist rule. At the conclusion of the 1989 Revolution, the first thought of the ethnic Germans was to flee Romania. The German government offered them full citizenship, even though they had been absent eight hundred years. By the thousands they abandoned ship until few remained in Romania. Entire villages emptied out, leaving huge, cathedral-like churches standing vacant.

The population of Transylvania, discounting the Gypsies and few remaining Germans, stands at about 50/50 Romanian-Hungarian. Controlled ethnic tensions roil under the surface as the ethnic Hungarians, even after more than eighty years, resent being under Romanian rule. This is exacerbated by the fact that Romania remains backward economically while prosperity holds sway in Hungary.

Targu Mures, with a population of some 180,000, sits in the middle of Transylvania. It is a clean city, and it was here that John brought us from the turmoil of Bucharest to a new life.

After moving the project to Transylvania, John's wife, Deana, soon joined him. A large house was built—and that is where John's story intersects mine.

John extended his hand of help to many boys and girls. Some refused, some accepted and then left, while others remained and are part of the "family" to this day. As the boys grew toward adulthood, John began to work in Gypsy villages helping the poor and their children. It was his hope that his boys would follow in his footsteps serving the poor. That is in its establishment stage at this time.

One evening at prayer time the boys asked John, "You had many other children you cared for in Japan, the United States and Honduras. What was the difference between them and us?"

John thought for a moment and then replied, "They all called me Brother John. You call me Daddy!"

CHAPTER 18

A Place of Respect

In November of 1994 a boy named Remus returned to our gang after an absence of several months. He had been at "Daddy's place" in Targu Mures. He told us all about conditions in that project—what a tremendous place it was, but he never said a word about why he left there. Despite the remarkable picture he painted of the place, it made no difference to me because I had no interest in going there or even trying to get in.

Around the same time other bigger boys returned from Targu Mures and, in conversation with members of our gang, gave the same positive account as Remus had. They said the conditions were good; there were two or three boys to a room, and the food was excellent. The real problem was that the boys were not allowed to smoke, and, being a strict regimen, they were also not allowed to use bad language, fight or insult one another. In addition, they

121

had to ask permission to do anything or go anywhere.

A fifteen-year-old that John had taken in had run off back to Bucharest. This boy had a very bad past. When he was ten, he had killed a small girl and been expelled from his village. He stayed drugged almost day and night trying to forget who he was. Once back in Bucharest he realized that for the first time in his life someone had cared about him deeply as a person and it made no difference what he had done in the past. When the reality of that hit him, he called John and asked to be taken back.

It was broadcast throughout the Gara that on January 5, John would be coming down from Transylvania to take Bobi "home." That was how I met John for the first time.

I talked with him, although I knew I had no chance of getting into his project. The other boys who had returned from there were the ones that convinced me of that. Therefore I didn't even try to make a good impression— nor was he impressed with me. I acted goofy, not realizing he appreciated those who were serious.

He left to go back to Targu Mures after giving me some money to buy bread for all the boys in my gang. Nevertheless, in the depths of my being I began to hope that somehow I would have a chance to escape from the streets through this man.

Thirteen days passed. Then I heard that John would be coming back to Bucharest on January 18. I don't know why, but I was afraid to meet with him.

January 18 came. That morning I went to buy two bottles of aurolac and returned to the Gara around 11 o'clock. I wasn't drugged yet, but I expected to be before long. One of the gang, Nelu, came along and told me that when John's train arrived he usually took the boys that met him to a restaurant. Nelu and some others were going to be there, and if I wanted, I could tag along and join them.

The train arrived, and eight of us went to eat. Afterward, half the group left, and I was invited to stay with the rest and join in a discussion. In that moment I had to make a decision: go back to the Gara and get drugged (I had the two bottles in my pocket), or go with them. I don't know why I was afraid of the situation, but, anyhow, I decided at once to go with John and the little gang that was with him. I gave the two bottles of aurolac to Nelu as I left. I still didn't believe I had any chance of going to Targu Mures.

There were about four or five of us. We were separated and talked to individually. A lot of questions were put to me, and I responded with the absolute truth. Finally John decided to take me with him to Transylvania. I didn't know whether to be happy or sad. I kept thinking, *Well, I'm going up there, but what if I return here?*

We all walked back together to the Gara. I insisted on taking John to the "basement" to show him where we lived. I told all the others that I was leaving, and they were surprised at my decision. I went for a moment to see my friend Catalin who lived in one of the apartments over the Gara and had often given me advice. When I told him of my decision, he said, "You'll be back, Vagabond." I told him, "No, I'll be staying!"

We took the night train and arrived in Targu Mures in the early morning. It had turned bitter cold in the night, and all the taxis were in service. John tried to order a cab, but the dial on the phone at the station was frozen—so we had to wait an hour for a bus. After what seemed like a year we arrived at John's house. It was beautiful and large: three stories, twelve rooms, plus three rooms in the basement. It had just been constructed especially for the street kids and lived in only seven weeks. The house was clean, as were all the boys. I was not used to seeing so many clean kids and thought they looked handsome, especially since they also looked content.

We ate—and I was so hungry! After breakfast I was given a haircut. My head was full of lice, and it embarrassed me. Then I took a bath, was given clothes and shown the room and bed I would occupy. Thus I entered the "Fundatia Familia Copiilor" (Children's Family Foundation).

The first month was fairly uncomplicated. Nothing much happened. I listened to music, ate and played various games with the other boys.

That house was different from any other that I had ever known. The whole system was different. The foundation of everything was, "I respect you. You respect me!" I learned this right from the beginning. We attempted to be a real family. So there were we boys, Daddy and his wife, Deana, whom we called "Mommy."

The boys that had returned to the Gara said the program was strict, but to me, it didn't seem to be so in the least. I couldn't figure out what they had been talking about.

At this point I was fifteen and a half years old. In

February, a few weeks after I arrived, I started to school. It was a bit difficult getting back into the habit of school after an absence of one and a half years, but little by little, all I had learned in the past began to come back to me. Thus I adjusted rapidly to my classes. Another boy in the home, Cristi, went to school with me. Now I had something to do besides just pass time, and that was study for school.

Daddy and Mommy were people who lived for God. No matter what it was, they tried to be an example to us in everything. From time to time we would study the Bible together. The custom was to get together two or three times a week to read the Bible and discuss what Jesus said. I respected Daddy for this. At the core, I had somehow, even in Bucharest, gained a fear of God, and what Daddy was now teaching me reinforced it. For me, this simple fact of reading the Bible together helped me a lot.

All my life I had a respect for God even though I knew little about Him. I had never had any evidence presented to me that He existed; nevertheless, deep in my soul there was something that effected a fear of Him.

My parents never talked to me about those private matters that had to do with faith. It was my observation that my father was totally indifferent. I knew that my mother believed in God, but she only went to the Orthodox Church now and then.

Not knowing God or anything about Him, when I did pray I prayed to an unknown God. I had heard something about Jesus, that He was God's Son, but nothing else. In reality, we were heathens. There was no foundation in me for a conscience, and therefore I had no regret whatsoever for all the evil things I did. What little guiding conscience I did have was based on some undefined influence that was passed to me from my mother.

I remember that in our house we had an icon showing Jesus being baptized by John the Baptizer and a dove descending upon His head. I gazed at that icon many times. I tried to understand the expression on Jesus' face and fathom the meaning of the halo surrounding Him. I was badly confused and could deduce nothing.

When I was out on the streets, in my desperation I prayed after some fashion almost every night to this unknown God. I asked Him for three things: a job, a wife and children, and that I escape from the streets.

Prayer does not pass vacuously into the air. It is clear now that God was listening and heard my prayer for three reasons. It was from my heart; it was in my own words; and I was sincere. So, my prayers were heard and I was given a new home, especially one where Bible principles were put into practice: a Christian family. When I entered that family the desires of the street remained behind. I lost all appetite for drugs and cigarettes, and I lost the desire to curse and insult others. It was as if I had been born again into a new world and a new life. It was a world that was not tainted with the depravity of the street, but a peaceful world that I could enjoy without shame. Most of all, it was an environment where I could perceive God.

Over time, I began to know God in a factual sense. I could feel His love for me, and I could understand the Bible, which I had been unable to comprehend in the past.

Thus, drawing nearer to God and having people around

me from whom I could gain example and inspiration, my behavior changed. I now had principles by which to live and a new conscience that had been awakened. I understood that God wanted to help me and that Jesus living in me could effect the changes that had to take place to erase the atrocity of the past and set me on the path to productivity. These changes did not take place slowly, over time, but they seemed to tumble one upon another until the day that I stopped to look back at where I had been and compared it to where I was now—and realized I had become a Christian in the fullest sense of the word. I could not live by my own efforts, but only by the transforming power that came from God Himself.

Now I knew the difference between good and evil. At that point I had to repent for all the evil I had done in the past so that it could be atoned for and erased. I was happy I did not have to pay for my own sins. Jesus had done it for me.

As I had already known when living in the streets, it was senseless to attempt to understand the meaning of life while in that condition. Life under those circumstances had no meaning. The greatest artistic masterpiece in the world has no meaning in a dark room.

In regard to that, I must clarify that the painting may have "value" in the dark, but it has no "meaning" without light. In the same way, the street children are not without value as many might think. It is just that there is no meaning to their existence while they are living in the darkness. Because they have value, a few are willing to sacrifice their lives to help them.

Some have envisioned Jesus coming to the big city. Instead of heading for the largest church in town, He goes out on the streets to mix with humanity. He views the street children; He views the elderly street people whose nameless faces have long been forgotten by whatever family they may have had; He views an endless series of other sorrows and injustices—and He weeps! He weeps and will not be comforted for He did not come to be inspired by the reverent and respectable in their churches, but He came to see what His servants are doing to fulfill His command to rescue the lost and suffering.

One thing that was hard to comprehend was that Daddy actually respected us boys. It was not hard to understand that he was friendly; it was a little more difficult to realize he had affection for us; but respect? People had always looked down on us as trash—the lowest dregs of society. Daddy wanted us to feel that we were someone special. It made no difference what we had done; he had the same respect for all of us—even the boy prostitutes and the one who had committed murder.

Sundays we went to church. We were not required to go—it was voluntary. I think it was that freedom to choose that made us all want to go. We sang songs and listened to preaching. I really began to feel more human—as if I really did have some value. I could see and understand that Jesus came also for me. Daddy emphasized strongly Jesus' love for the poor and outcasts.

The fact that I now had enough food, along with attentive care, destroyed every last vestige in me of the desire for aurolac. From the day I left the Gara until today I never

touched drugs again. I have no explanation other than it
was with the help of God.

I got along beautifully with the other boys in the house.
They saw that my comportment was good, so I came to be
trusted and accepted.

A few months later, in April, I asked permission one day
to go take a walk. I hadn't smoked in three and a half
months, and now the craving for a cigarette overwhelmed
me. As I walked down the street all I could think of was a
smoke. Then I saw a butt lying on the ground right in
front of me. I picked it up and lit it. I took a few drags off
of what was left and threw the rest away. I was filled with
such shame over what I had done I turned around and
went straight back to the house, to Daddy's office, and
said, "Daddy, I smoked! I'm really sorry." I promised I
would never do it again. He neither scolded me nor condemned me. Even though he had told us all not to smoke,
he now freely forgave me. I told him the problem was that
I found I still had the craving for nicotine. He said we
needed to ask God's help, and he prayed with me. From
that day to this, five years later, I have never picked up
another cigarette.

CHAPTER 19

Healing Inner Wounds

Until June 1995 everything at the home was in reference to me; that is, my physical condition improved greatly, I gained weight and grew in height. It was not an exception but normal to be clean all the time and dressed in clean clothes. I was content. In addition to my physical state, a healing was beginning to take place inside: a healing of all the wounds I received in the past and the bad experiences of living in the streets.

In Bucharest, what occupied virtually all my time was survival. I concentrated exclusively on what would satisfy my physical needs: begging and searching for food and drugs. Now, none of those things were necessary. Food and clothing were provided, recreation was available, and I had a soft bed to sleep in. Survival was no longer a problem.

Therefore, physically I was fine, but the wounds in the interior and the pain caused by them began to rise to the surface. At the same time, I realized that something could be made of my life, but I was afraid of the analysis and probing that would be necessary to achieve stability. I had had nothing but problems since I was seven years old: seven and a half years out on the streets, rejected by my parents, aimless, socially maladjusted and leading the life of a young criminal. My whole life had been concentrated on the issue of survival—how to stay alive. Now all of this had changed.

Until the age of seven I was a child, but then, until I was fifteen I was in an adult world—a world of the mature. Thus, I never had an adolescence. Nevertheless, even though I was now fifteen, in my emotions, sentiments, desires and in my heart I still wanted to be a child. I was cut to the core by any insult another boy threw my way, and, like a child, I was thirsty for affection. I dreamed about things a child would dream about and wanted things a child would want—but on the outside, I was a man. I wanted to be hugged and kissed like a child— things I had never experienced in my life.

So this was the condition I was in. My wounds ran deep. They manifested themselves in feelings of loneliness, rejection and depression. All my life I had been alone, so even now I was beginning to retreat back into isolation. I didn't like to hang around with the other boys, nor did I want to have to open up in front of other people.

Because of the fact that society did not want me and that the attitude of people toward me when I was in the streets was bad, now, because of that past rejection, I transferred it onto those around me and began to feel rejected by them, too. Since I felt people didn't like me, coupled with having lived years in the streets, I had a negative opinion of myself. If someone said, "You are a very nice boy," I would think, *Go on! Leave me alone! Can't you see how ugly I am?*

If I had a problem with someone, I would back out of it immediately. I always had the instinct of retreating when someone tried to hurt me. I never wanted to be hurt again and would do anything to avoid it.

With all these complications inside of me, God sent me a good friend with whom I could talk. It was the first time in my life to open up in front of anyone. This friend was an American girl, older than I, who had come to Romania to help with the girls' unit of John's project. (He had also taken eight girls out of the Gara. Like the boys, not all stayed.) I told her everything about my past.

I found it very hard to accept myself—the fact that I was a man. I accepted the fact that someday I would get married and have children, but I found it very hard to imagine that such a thing could actually happen.

I had hurt many in the past also, and I was afraid of doing it again. I couldn't imagine how one so damaged as I was could ever love a girl. What would she say about being friends with someone who had been at the bottom—lived in the streets, ate garbage? Many times I thought of myself as a beast wanting a beauty for a girlfriend.

Thus, in June 1995, with the help of God, I began to fight against these negative feelings in my life. The injuries went very deep. In my whole life no one had ever told me that they loved me.

As time went by I realized I needed a mother, so I drew very close to Mommy, the director's wife. Inasmuch as she taught me how to be more open, I started to be more open. We began to talk every evening about whatever subject arose. She showed genuine appreciation for my abilities and for just what I was as a person. That was something new. I also began to learn English together with her.

One evening when I was really depressed, I talked with her, and she made it clear that she was willing to be a mother to me. Then she said something I had never heard in my life, "I love you!" With tears in my eyes I looked at her, not understanding fully what had happened and still questioning, "Who, me? Me, loved?" But I accepted the love and affection she offered, and it was a big step forward.

It was more difficult for me to establish a father-son relationship with Daddy because of the twisted relationship I had had with my own father. But that too was resolved in time.

The wounds inside did not remain hidden. They came to the surface and stood in front of me. For the amount of pain that was in me, to be healed would take anyone years and years. For me to become normal, in the sense I thought of as normal, took almost three years.

There were other kids, both in the project and in the Gara, who never fought against their pain. They allowed it to overwhelm them and then covered it over. Perhaps it was too painful to face their past and present problems, so they put a blanket over everything to hide the rubbish that was in there. What was different in me that I cared about my condition? I don't know. All I do know is that I wanted to confront it and be free of the terrible burden I was carrying. In Bucharest, though I looked like a hardened, junior criminal, in my heart I was really soft, compassionate and thirsty for affection.

And now, I thought, what would I do when I had my own family? Would I make the same mistakes my own mother and father had made? No! I would learn something from their mistakes. I would be loving to my wife and to my children. Just because I never received any love didn't mean my own children had to suffer the same fate. I would offer them my love and affection. I had already thought much about it, and I determined that I would make time every day to sit down and talk with my children—talk about their problems and their joys. We would have a strong relationship established upon respect and love. This is the most important manner in which a child should grow up.

CHAPTER 20

Questions
I Can't Answer

We have no real idea of how fine-tuned the life of a child is. It was God's intention when children were created dependent upon their parents that they should be raised in an atmosphere of love and acceptance that, in turn, leads to stability and functional maturity. Total chaos results when this plan is interrupted or lacking. Children from alcoholic families are disturbed in one way, children from otherwise dysfunctional families in other ways. The ultimate disturbance is the total alienation of a child from his past, present or future—and at that point, he or she hits the streets and becomes a non-person.

One day John asked a depressed-looking teenage street boy outside the Gara, "How can I help you? Is there anything I can do for you?"

The boy replied, "We have no idea of how we can be

helped."

John persisted, "But what about the future?"

The boy answered, "We know nothing of the future."

This is the ultimate in detachment from society and reality.

As already mentioned, I was reared the first seven years of my life free. After that I moved into the city and another kind of life—and I spent the next eight years searching and longing for that life of liberty. Perhaps I owe the fact that I was able to escape from eight years of bondage to those first seven years of my life spent in freedom with my grandmother. It put a foundation under me that still remained after all the rubble of a life in ruins was cleared away. Now, five years later, I have changed so much it doesn't seem as if I were ever on the streets. It is as if it were something I dreamed, some kind of nightmare that vanished upon awaking in the morning sun.

My whole thinking has changed. Instead of being self-centered (which is the desire only to get and get), now I want to give: give love, respect and whatever I can to others who need it. I made my peace with society.

So many memories, so many stories, so much suffering. Some of it now makes me laugh, and some the passage of time has turned into pleasant memories. Others still leave tears in my eyes and leave me sad.

I asked myself many times, "Did I really have to go through all I went through? Was it really necessary to fulfill some mystical purpose—the abuse, the beatings, the hunger, the misery? Why wasn't I born into a normal family?" Only God has the answer to all of this.

Then the companion question comes, "Why was it only I who was chosen to escape from my gang?" It would seem to be divine favor. Many others had the same chance, but many threw it away. I had the chance, and I grasped it.

Now, several years later, it is interesting to note what has happened to the old gang. Some are still derelicts, puffing away on their bag of aurolac. How they have managed to survive years of this kind of abuse I don't know. It is not only the aurolac but everything that goes with it: insufficient food, eating garbage, the cold in winter, unsanitary conditions, going for months without a bath and being covered with lice.

Others of the old gang had many chances to be rehabilitated, but they chose their freedom over a disciplined situation that would lead to a stable future. Many of those who chose freedom are now in prison. Others have suffered great tragedies. Some died. One became a legend when he had his arm cut off upon reaching for his winnings after a poker game, and one was run over by a train. Another lost both hands trying to steal a live, 20,000-volt electric line. Others aimlessly wander the streets hardly having what one could call a life.

John has lost count of the number of children he attempted to rescue. A few tried to pull themselves out. They took advantage of facilities available to them and attempted to get some education. Some have already made it. Like ghosts from the past, several have called John when he least expected it and said, "Daddy, I just want you to know I made it. I broke free. I have a responsible job now, I'm living in a good apartment, and my future is secure. I wasn't one of those who stayed with you all the way, but you took me off the streets and got me started in the right direction." And for John, that's good enough.

We hold our breath watching others struggle and are reminded of an individual sinking into quicksand, an arm and hand extended above the mire in a plea for rescue. It is only the ones who know they are sinking that can be pulled out.

Those who work with street children have a difficult task. Many kids, in their instability, run away again and again from facilities established to assist them. A few exhibit extreme antisocial behavior, and all street kids are, to one extent or another, antisocial. That arises from being "unbonded" children. They cannot attach to anyone. In most cases the parents are responsible for the syndrome, but the child is blamed for it.

The normal state for a child is to be bonded to his parents. The bonding takes place in infancy. Parents in affluent countries who drop their infant offspring off at day-care centers risk ending up with an unbonded child who may exhibit varying degrees of antisocial behavior later on. The more he is bonded, the more stable and secure the child is. It is rare for a bonded child to take off for the streets unless he is abandoned or the victim of abnormal circumstances. If he does end up in the streets, he is one of those that workers will point to with pride as an example of their rehabilitative skills. Let them have the same results with a real sociopathic child, and they would have, indeed, something to crow about.

Some workers who came to help had stars in their eyes,

not understanding what they were really dealing with, and they folded early in the game and slipped back to their home country, their optimism extinguished. The average street kid is so badly damaged he does not want to be rescued. He wants to be helped, but not rescued. He is first of all working out the hurt and pain in his life. And if the pain cannot be assuaged, he cannot move on to the next step of stability. It is very rare that someone in great pain can lead a normal life. Therefore, it requires great patience on the part of those who attempt to minister to the street children and also a bit of experimentation to find what works. Many workers are criticized when their experiments misfire, but as an old saying goes, "It is better to try and fail than to do nothing and succeed." But trying to bond an unbonded child is a bit like trying to glue something to an oily surface.

When I said the average kid wants to be helped but not rescued, I mean he wants a sandwich today, but not to be pulled into a long-term structured situation. Many coming from abroad, thinking they can clean up the whole street kid situation overnight, have been misled by the enthusiasm and gratitude with which a child will accept a sandwich. They report this back home as conclusive success. Others, knowing that many street kids exist as parasites and do not want rehabilitation, have criticized those who have persisted in carrying food to them without expecting a positive response in return. It is much like the Christian evangelists who will not preach unless they are guaranteed some converts. But the kindness of continuing to feed the children, even without apparent results, must continue. Jesus never told His followers that the hungry should be fed only if they respond. The act of kindness itself has its effect. Of course, feeding the unresponsive does not seem as spectacular as feeding those who will kiss one's feet.

John began a daily journal the day he arrived in Romania and has continued it to the present day. He comments, "Anyone looking into my diary expecting to find a thrilling day-by-day account of rescuing street children would be stunned. It is, rather, a narrative of defeats, disappointments, unbelievable betrayals (not only from street kids), discouragements, frustrations, obstacles, criticisms and weariness. Scattered among these are the few successes that have made it all worthwhile. It has definitely been panning for gold: much effort expended and tons of sand processed to gain a few precious flakes."

I was one of those gained, and my thanks extend to those who had the persistence to work long enough to separate me from the mire I was in. My admiration extends to all those, Romanian and foreign, who came with love and patience in their hearts.

CHAPTER 21

The Remains
of My Family

Six months after I was rescued out of the Gara I had
to return to Buzau to retrieve my personal documents. As already mentioned, my grandmother had
died in 1993, and, meanwhile, my parents had moved out
of the city and into her house. Both my parents were
shocked beyond belief at my improved appearance. Not
only they, but all those neighbors who had last seen me
working for my Uncle Dumitru were likewise astounded.
My father, having learned nothing, wanted to force me to
stay, but my mother said that if they couldn't persuade me
to stay, "Let him go!" Of all the things my mother ever
said or did, this was the best and wisest.

I have been back to visit again since. It seems that often
we do not need to wait for divine retribution. Those who
sin against us punish themselves. So, things have not gone
well for my father. He no longer works but spends his days

in idleness and drinking; his bottle of wine is his only close companion. Two years ago he went on a rampage in the apartment, smashed all the furniture and threw the TV over the balcony to the pavement below. The police came and hauled him off to the same mental institution he had put me in. The doctors told him if he kept up his same rate of drinking he would not live to see fifty. So he cut down a little, but could not stop altogether. Thus, the discipline he once imposed on me he cannot impose upon himself. He is withdrawn and in despair, so my three brothers and my sister seem oblivious to him if not disrespectful. The household is chaotic and the children undisciplined. My mother only waits for some motive to divorce him. All my father's venom appears to have been expended on me. In retrospect I would have to say what Joseph, in Genesis, said to his brothers, "[He] meant it for evil. God meant it for good."

My father has had a lot of time to think—five years since I first went back a new person. He now regrets all the evil he did to me. It can be forgiven but not undone. He wants me back, but there is no way that can happen. The destiny God has for me now does not match his. If I were to remain there, I would end up a simple shepherd spending my life watching over herds of foolish sheep.

My future is to put something into society: to change something, to help someone, to make a difference. I am willing to sacrifice my life for anything that I know will make a difference. I want to be a productive citizen. I was nothing, but now I have value. I was lost, but now I am on a path going somewhere.

AFTERWORD

As Catalin concluded his story, he told me that it was as if it happened thirty or forty years ago to someone else, not just a scant five years before. So many incredible things have happened since. The boy who failed first grade has won a commendation three years in a row for being the top student in his class.

Business in Romania, even nonprofit charitable work, is extremely complicated due to the bureaucracy. Thus every organization has an administrator. When our administrator became permanently incapacitated, Catalin took over the difficult job and has done it very efficiently. We are planning for Catalin to take over the entire project eventually.

In June of 2000, Catalin, Alex (to be mentioned later) and I were invited to Washington, D.C. to meet with Senator Mary Landrieu of Louisiana. With an active interest in Romanian children's affairs, the senator wanted to hear firsthand from the boys their experiences and opinions. She scheduled ninety minutes, a lot of time for a senator, and took us to eat in the historic Senate dining room.

Since I think of Catalin as a son, I have begun making other provisions for him. He has been an invaluable help to me, and though I have forty years more experience working with children than he does, I lean heavily on him for advice and counsel. Who knows better than he the mentality and needs of the down and out?

I was deeply moved on my birthday in October 1999 to receive a card with the following handwritten message:

> What can I say to a man who helped me so much, except, "Thank you, Dad, and Happy Birthday!!!" Gold and silver I don't have, but what I have I'll give you, and that is my respect, my admiration, my love for you for all that you've done for me through the years. I will stand by you in everything, helping you and being faithful in all of my ways. Catalin

Those few lines should tell you the kind of person he is, how far he has come and where he is going. There doesn't seem to be much more I can add to that.

JMK

Religion and the Street Child

Religion and the Christian
Sources of the Problem
by JMK

I t is hard to say whether the average street child has a
religion or not. Considering their criminal activities,
one might write them off altogether as heathens.
Whatever, their consciences are disconnected from their
actions and from such beliefs as they might have.

Basically, they live in despair. They have heard of God
but are not sure He exists—though they tend to believe
He does. They have heard of heaven and hell but have no
proof such places exist.

They have no real idea of who Jesus is. Some who come
from strong Orthodox homes might fare better on that
subject. But even they do not seem to know that Jesus died
for their sins, much less that He exists as a reality and that
He loves them. Like the general public, they believe good
works produce some merit, but it matters little to them

because they have no good works.

Religious art is displayed in public places and portrays Jesus, but it does little to enlighten because He is depicted as a figure with whom no one can identify. Eastern art especially endows Jesus with a mystical, even mythical quality that hardly conveys reality.

A few pray. It was doubtlessly Catalin's sincere prayers that rescued him from his situation. But for most, God has no part in their lives. Living only for the present, they cannot see ahead far enough to conceive of a program of divine reward or retribution. The aesthetic liturgies that inspire many are meaningless to them and say nothing to their misery.

When I first came to Romania and spoke in a few Romanian churches, I shocked the churchgoers by saying, "I appreciate the worship and music here. I appreciate that you have a church family and that Jesus is here with you.

"But as for me, Jesus said, 'Where I am, there shall my servant be also.' For me, Jesus is not here. He is in Bucharest with the street children. My church is the Gara de Nord, and that's where I worship." Some understood, but others couldn't grasp the concept.

Religion tends to lag behind social change. Many Christian workers are still operating on a methodology decades old—if not centuries. Whatever contempt is directed toward some Christian workers is based on the observation that the worker is out of touch with reality. Young prostitutes, whether girl or boy, are not going to be rehabilitated by telling them that what they are doing is sinful and they need to be saved—to get right with God. There was a time when that might have meant something, but the issue today is far more complex. Such statements are meaningless today because there is no foundation under them either of religion or morality.

When the woman caught in the act of adultery was brought to Jesus (John chapter 8), she did not need to be told that what she was doing was wrong. The value system of her day taught her that. In a similar way, older workers, such as myself, grew up in a time when all young people believed in God and went to church. Their world-view and morality were shaped by their church; it made no difference what the denomination. In 1960, when I last worked as a camp counselor, we could assume that all children believed in God, knew who Jesus was, what He taught, and knew the Ten Commandments as the foundation for morality. All further teaching was built on top of that foundation.

That situation no longer exists. Most children nowadays no longer know the Ten Commandments, and their concept of God is obscure. Workers with whom I am in contact in the United States are reporting that they come in contact increasingly with children who have never heard of Jesus except as a curse word. They have never been in a church and have no idea of what goes on in one.

If the matter just stopped there it would be one thing, but the reality is that the modern child's world-view and value system are learned from television and films—a value system that is not amoral but immoral. If it were amoral now, as it was in its early days, there would be no complaint. But television has taken over from the churches the role as the shaper of the child's moral system. If the older generation would understand this, they would be less mystified by the increase in aberrant behavior among the youth.

Since television no longer places any restraint on speech, the foundation of culture has also been severely eroded, for culture is the gracious use of language. The language in films and on TV nowadays is anything but gracious.

After saying all that, I will have to qualify that in some areas, the church still exerts a significant influence. Since there are a large number of street children now in the United States and gangs are a menace to the citizenry, we would have to say that the two value systems exist almost side by side, running on parallel tracks.

When we look, however, at a country such as Romania with its street child population of virtual heathen, we can understand the failure of religion to say anything significant at all to the child struggling in pain in a modern world. It is not that religion, i.e., Christianity, *has* nothing to say. It does! But it is not saying it in a way that conveys any meaning or significance to the present-day child. The modern child needs what Christianity has to offer; that is why it is such a tragedy. A telephone, no matter how expensive or well built, will not communicate when the wires are down.

Catalin found everything he ever wanted after connecting with God. Others too could be brought up out of their despair. Christian workers have what the street child needs. They need to communicate it, not in archaic terms but in language the child can understand, relate to and use as a base to build upon. In addition, perhaps less preaching and more action would convey a practical message. When I brought new children into our home I never confronted them directly with religion. Religion was a very natural and especially practical part of our lives; it was not a theological concept but something the child could comprehend and say, "Hey, I need that." So, we ate, we worked, we slept and we believed. It was all a natural part of living and not a forced "now we are going to pray" kind of thing.

A great need in Romania, or other places with a street child problem, is for compassionate workers. Frankly, it is a major problem that founders of projects generally cannot find staff that are anything but indifferent to the children.

When I was running a feeding program in the Gara de Nord, I was desperate for workers. I went to the largest evangelical seminary in Bucharest and offered a salary to any student who would spend ninety minutes an evening feeding children. After all, college students all over the world are looking for easy employment. To my amazement not one student was interested—neither for love nor money. They could find no correlation between their intent to become pastors and the suffering of the poor within a few yards of them.

Therefore, Christianity must be more than liturgy and symbols and pious talk. That is what James meant when he wrote, "Faith without works is dead." Catalin, other boys in our home and I myself searched for years to find a faith that is alive, accompanied by good deeds. It is our wish to do what Jesus would do if He were here today, and we hope to influence others to do the same.

The street children's world of suffering is the real world and the only world for them. Any religion they have would need to fit into the reality of that system. Because of that, heaven is a concept without meaning. One might suspect hell would be better understood, but their hell is now and the police their personal devils.

When one really understands what forty-five years of Communism meant, it is not hard to understand why the Romanian public is so indifferent to the plight of those who are suffering. At the top of the list during the Communist era was personal safety and survival. One's friendly neighbor could be an informant for the secret police. One's pious priest and confessor could also be reporting your every fault to the authorities. It is estimated that as high as 90 percent of the Orthodox priests were working for the secret police. Every Baptist and Pentecostal congregation also contained at least one informant, if not more. Even one's own child could say something at school that would end up on a police desk.

The whole system had quite an effect. When I arrived, three years after the Revolution, people still walked in public with their eyes averted. That has changed now.

So people withdrew into their personal world and wrapped a cloak tighter than a shepherd's sheepskin around them. Anyone and everyone could be a dangerous enemy. One would hardly, then, care about a street child.

Even the evangelical Christians had the compassion

sucked right out of them. Not only were they under sur-
veillance in their churches and, therefore, as much on
guard, if not more so, than anyone else, but the government took the place of God. People in the West could not
understand why the Communists hated religion so much.
It was because they wanted no competition, especially
from God. They would build a new society that was perfect and, in accordance with their humanistic pride,
needed no outside help. One woman told me, "They kept
harping on it incessantly. We had to listen to it day and
night how they were doing all this for *us*!" Therefore, only
the government was allowed to engage in social works. It
was supposed to be a perfect society: no poverty, the elderly cared for, even the handicapped supported. The reality was that in the norm, the system worked. But too
often, outside the norm, the system broke down. In certain segments of society the poverty and suffering were
extreme. As Catalin pointed out, Ceausescu mandated five
children to a family, but five children were more than a
family could support, and the excess spilled out into the
orphanages and streets. The social engineering of the
Communists was a colossal disaster from which it will take
decades to recover. In fact, I don't believe there will ever be
recovery unless more students are educated in the West.

So the stage was set. Personal interest was paramount.
Beggars were parasites because they were supposed to be
supported by the State and not bring disgrace upon the
socialist society by their unkempt, offending presence.
Street children were totally outside the system. Not even
the Communists knew what to do with them except beat

them and send them home; and anything the Communists could not control was an extreme frustration to them.

After the Revolution, the discipline went out of society. People had new predicaments to deal with. They didn't know what to make of the street children and wished they would go away.

On my first trip to Romania I carried sandwiches several times to the children living in the Gara de Nord and then made known my long-range plans. A lay pastor came to me with an interpreter—quite upset.

"You should know something about these street children you are helping," he began. "They are dirty, they are thieves, they smoke, they are immoral, they use aurolac. And you want to help children like that? You carry food to them and want to give them clothing. My own children were in want when they were growing up. Why should these filthy street kids have anything that my own children did not have?"

It was very well stated. And I will have to add that, to the man's credit, a year later after he had seen what I had done, he apologized for his attitude. However, he expressed the attitude of the public in general. And until they see things differently and change their attitude, social problems such as the street child phenomenon will not be resolved. It will take a bit more compassion and understanding. No child comes into existence by himself. Society itself gave birth to the street child, and now it wants to make him a bastard.

So, looking at him sprawled on the sidewalk with his

bag of aurolac or sitting against the wall in the train station, one might see only a grime-covered, drugged, revolting figure. How he got in that condition is not obvious. A thieving street kid? He had his family, affection and childhood stolen from *him*! A drugged disgrace? How could he help but seek solace in any form available that would help him forget his circumstances? Imagine passing the ages of six, seven, eight or nine all alone out on the streets. The public may view him with distaste, but there are those walking around in plain daylight who should be incarcerated for putting him there.

Thus, I never told a child he was a sinner who ought to repent for stealing, for immorality, for prostitution, for drugs or whatever other unpalatable activity he was engaged in. I have watched several well-meaning workers grabbing the bags of aurolac from children or setting their bags of aurolac on fire. I have watched them snatch the cigarettes out of children's mouths, saying, "You don't want that anymore!" I never did that! The crime committed against that child must be atoned for first. How can that child understand the love of Jesus if I don't love him first? The grime and deplorable condition these children are in never repelled me, and I have been closer to their lice than I indicated in the preface. But after all public opinion has been expressed, the fact remains that the children are the victims, not the guilty. Whether or not they want our religion depends on how we live it before them.

I am reminded of Psalm 69. If anything expresses the despairing wail of a street child it is this psalm.

Save me, O God, for I am in water up to my neck. I am sinking deep into the mud with nowhere to stand. I have ended up in deep water with a torrent washing over me. I am weary with my crying; my throat is dry. My eyes fail while I wait for my God. Those who hate me without a cause are more than the hairs of my head. Those who would destroy me are powerful. Though I have stolen nothing, do I still have to repay it?* You [O God] know my reproach, my shame, my dishonor; my adversaries are all known to you. Reproach has broken my heart. I am dejected and depressed. I looked for someone to take pity on me, but there was no one; and for comforters but there were none.

—Paraphrased

*In other words, "Though my parents sinned against me, though they stole from me my life, my family, and my childhood, I am the one accused, and society demands of me that I repay what was taken from me and pay for the crimes I commit to survive."

Appendix B

Sociopaths: Two Case Studies
by JMK

Any person working with street children, or attempting to work with them, should be aware that a majority of them are sociopaths (also called psychopaths). Sociopaths display antisocial behavior that is usually cleverly concealed. What is so misleading is that they are quite normal except in matters that pertain to self-interest and gratification. Thus, they can perform a work task with an efficiency that evokes admiration; but, at the same time, they think nothing of cheating an elderly woman or robbing a blind man. They are master liars and usually lie even when the truth would better serve their purposes. They have no empathy with other humans. What is so dangerously deceiving about them to an unskilled worker encountering them on the street is an apparent sincerity and an affectionate warmth that melts the heart. By this skill, they disarm the unwary who, sooner or later, find themselves victims. Yet, so ingenious is the sociopath that the worker may not at first understand he or she is a victim and gets taken several times before the truth and reality of the situation dawns. And when it does, the inevitable consequence is an emotional shock: that this beautiful child (or young adult) could have behaved thus and betrayed the trust and affection of the worker. Upon reflection, however, the worker returns to a position of "there is no such thing as a bad boy": that he has a mission to save this child, causing an increased output of energy and resources in an attempt to bring the boy or girl into conformity. This output of energy is usually wasted, how-ever, and detracts from those whom the worker could be reaching, who would be amenable to his efforts.

Although I have been working with youth forty-five years, I first began running into sociopaths in large numbers, like schools of fish, in the late 1980s in Honduras. I had estab-lished an orphanage and children's home in Honduras in 1976. My wife and I found the first years pleasant. We even adopted two boys who are now productive American citizens and of whom we can be proud. As time went on, however, I found less and less children coming into our project that were not socially disruptive. It finally came to the point where my entire project came to a halt.

At first I was unaware of what I faced. Other than hav-ing heard the term, I had no experience of what a sociopath was. Then, as though by the guidance of divine providence, I came across the book *High Risk: Children Without a Conscience* by Dr. Ken Magid and Carole A.

McKelvey (Bantam Books, 1989). It changed my whole perception. I have since recommended the book to other childcare workers who have been equally enthusiastic and worn out their copies. My copies never wore out because I always found a worker, upon whom I took pity, who needed it worse than I did—and I bought another.

Dr. Magid points out that basically a sociopathic personality is caused by lack of bonding to a parent figure in early infancy. The mind of a child is quite fragile and sensitive in relation to its development. That is why it takes many adults the rest of their lives to straighten out damage done to them through rearing mistakes on the part of parents. If a child has no strong bond to a parent, it is doubtful he will have any kind of bond to society either. All his energies will then be turned inward and expended upon himself.

It is virtually unheard of for a street child to come from a home where he has two loving, devoted parents. The very fact of parental rejection is what pushes a child out into the streets in the first place. I often think that newspaper reporters who spend an evening in Bucharest and then write a tear-jerking article for the American or British press on the plight of the forlorn street child should be forced to spend a couple days tied to one of these young dears.

Not all sociopaths have the same degree of derangement, however. It can vary from mild to intense, and the general public meets more of them than they realize. Of course, a habitual criminal is obviously antisocial. But so is the slick, used-car salesman who cares little about the piece of junk he unloads on an unwary customer. In his case, his disorder is covered by a legitimate profession within which he operates quite efficiently—his affliction being the engine that drives him to success and a desk full of awards as salesman of the year.

I have taken care of many sociopathic children in the past dozen years, and, to be very frank, I wish I had met none of them. Life is too short. I worked seven years with one who is memorable, and almost as long with others. They hung on like chewing gum to the sole of a shoe until, mercifully, they themselves finally got tired of the game and moved on to wider and more lush pastures where they could fleece the world. When they desire, they have a knack of so attaching themselves to a project that it is impossible to dislodge them. They know intuitively, however, when they have gone too far, and then back off and become so helpful and cooperative it brings a tear to the eye. It is at this point (when the worker begins to think he has prevailed) that it is most dangerous, because when one is disarmed and unsuspecting, they will move in again for the "kill."

I will, herewith, present two brief case histories. One, named Robert, is representative of the failures. The other, Alex, is the only sociopath I know of that I ever, to some extent, rehabilitated (with an unusual amount of help from God), and even then, I sleep with one eye open.

ROBERT

Robert (not his real name) was born to a relatively well-to-do family. When the boy was two, the parents divorced. The father's side of the family had the money, and custody of the boy was awarded to the father. It would be almost sixteen years before the boy saw his mother again.

Why the father wanted the boy is unknown. He was a drunk, and he ignored the child. Not too long after the divorce, the father remarried. The stepmother was a cold woman who already had a daughter in her early teens. Both mother and daughter were jealous of Robert, but for different reasons. To the daughter, Robert was an intruder into her relationship with her mother. As for the step-mother, she learned that Robert had inherited some prop-erty from his grandfather. In fact, it was a most unusual arrangement. The grandfather had adopted Robert as his son, thus making Robert his own father's brother. Robert and his father had jointly inherited the property, and the stepmother wanted it all. She and the daughter began beating the boy at every opportunity, thinking that maybe he would go away.

It was around this time, at age five, that Robert was raped by an uncle. In Robert's case, it turned out to be almost a curse that he was unusually handsome. The vio-lation, coupled with the beatings, provided the fuel for his first attempt at running away. But he lived in an isolated area, and there was really nowhere a five-year-old could run away to.

That was resolved a year later when the stepsister sud-denly became friendly one day and suggested they take a train trip together. The trip was exciting at first, but then began to drag on until Robert wondered if it would ever end. Where were they going?

At last he fell asleep. When he awoke the train had

stopped and all the passengers had disembarked. He was alone in the famous Gara de Nord, Bucharest's main train station, and only six years old.

We have, then, a child who was traumatized at home and now faced living in the streets alone: the perfect culture medium for a sociopath. He had to learn to survive by theft and cleverness and to watch his own back.

A year after he arrived in Bucharest the Revolution broke out. Robert remembers standing outside the Gara watching an advancing line of soldiers and tanks and a large mob of people throwing stones and shouting deprecations. An order was given, and the tanks and soldiers fired. It seemed as if fifty people fell dead in an instant. Suddenly, Robert no longer wanted to be a spectator. There was a bus in front of the Gara with the door open. Robert jumped on, not caring where it went, and the bus sped out of the area. He rode to the north about twenty minutes before alighting, but almost at once, shooting erupted around him again. He ran for an apartment building and into the elevator. After the elevator passed the fourth floor, Robert hit the stop button. He felt that in that tomblike elevator he was safe. He sat with his head resting on his knees for a long time until he no longer heard the sound of gunfire. A few moments later the elevator came to rest at the ground floor. He opened the door, only to draw back in fright. Two soldiers, hearing the elevator coming down, stood ready with weapons pointed at the door. But when they saw he was only a child, they grabbed him and ran out of the building. There was a car out in the middle of the street, driverless, but with its motor running. The soldiers pushed Robert into the back seat, got in the front and sped north to the television-communications building, which was heavily under guard. The soldiers took Robert all the way to the roof, where they passed him to an officer who covered him with his greatcoat. There was much fighting down on the street. A soldier standing next to Robert was shot through the head and fell dead.

After three days the fighting stopped, and the officer took Robert to his own home where his wife and children received the boy warmly. But he was already a young sociopath, and true to his nature, a few days later he slipped out in the middle of the night from the security of the officer's apartment and made his way back to the bosom of the streets.

I first met Robert when he was eleven years old—already five years on the streets. He was, indeed, a handsome boy, but he was very quiet, his face expressionless, and he said hardly a word. I brought him home, where he proceeded to demolish the tranquility of our house. Upon reflection I remember he had three states: wild laughter, crying and dead silence. Just when I was trying to figure out what to do about him, he left. About a week later he came back on his own, stayed a few days and left again. This went on several times that year—and then I didn't see him again until he was fourteen. The reason he dropped out of our lives was that he found something profitable and, at the same time, pleasurable that occupied his full attention, and that was prostitution. His clients were exclusively foreigners, and he learned to speak excellent English. One of the foreign men made porn films of teenage boys, to sell in other countries, and Robert acted in several.

When he was fourteen, Robert showed up on my doorstep one day, unexpected. He was at that gangly, awkward stage. I had not the least idea of the debauchery he had been in the previous two years. He seemed very content with us and much calmer than before, yet a month later, as quietly as he came, he left—but not without stealing a wad of money out of my jacket pocket. True to form as a sociopath, he came when he wanted and left when he wanted. If he needed money, he helped himself to that, too.

I heard briefly that Robert was in a Christian project in Bucharest—but then nothing more until January 2000 when, without warning, he showed up on my doorstep again. He was now almost eighteen years old and so poised and sophisticated I kept trying to match him with the gangly fourteen-year-old I had known three years before.

When he quietly disappeared one day three months later with $100 he stole from my office, he left in his wake a trail of destruction that took months to sweep up and, at the time I am writing this, is still not altogether resolved. I have very strong standards of how I want my home run and my boys to act. But true to form, he rearranged the whole place to his liking, as painlessly and unnoticed as a mosquito sucking blood from its victim in the night. With all my experience with sociopaths, it wasn't entirely that I was unaware. One part of me knew that he was not sincere in his "affection" for me. Yet the act these thespians put on is so flawless it would take God Himself, Who cannot deceive or be deceived (so says the catechism), to sort it out. I also knew he was rearranging the standards of the home, but I could not see how or when it was happening. In retrospect, the most amazing item on the list was that he actually told me two days before he left that he was going to run away, but I didn't believe him.

My contacts in Bucharest located Robert about a week later sleeping in a building under construction; they reported back a few days later that the boy had tried to commit suicide but was revived.

I see the wasted life of a very intelligent young man—a life that at this point is going nowhere and has no purpose. If he had never been beaten, raped, mistreated and abandoned, he would today be a normal boy just finishing high school. As it is, Robert has only completed fourth grade.

There are many Christians who would cluck their tongues over this young man's escapades: a boy prostitute? Horrible! Porn film star? My God! And I didn't mention he had used heroin and was once hospitalized for alcohol intoxication. Robert was also the best pickpocket in Bucharest and a master thief. So there is quite a list against him. Yet, something nags at me. It is that verse in John 9:2. "Who sinned? This [young] man or his parents?"

I ask: Who will answer for all this mess in the Day of Judgment? A boy is cruelly thrust out of his family at age six. When he is supposed to be enjoying his childhood— those years when he is supposed to be developing social skills, receiving love and guidance from his parents and gaining a conscience to tell him right from wrong— during those years he is learning other things: dark, unsavory things. Someone is going to pay. And I can tell you this: Robert is not going to foot the entire bill alone.

What will happen to Robert in the judgment? Here is where I am so pleased that God did not make us judges. In fact, His express word to me when I came to Romania was, "Do not judge any of these children. Just help them!" Four days before he left, Robert sat in my office and accepted Jesus as his Savior. He confessed all his sins to me as a sign of repentance and then asked forgiveness through Jesus.

Now, what was that verse about the prostitutes going into the kingdom ahead of the Pharisees?

ALEX

Alex was born in Bucharest in December 1983. His mother was the mistress of a man who already had a wife and children on the other side of town. Alex was not supposed to happen, but abortions were illegal under the Communist regime.

When Alex was two, his parents had some kind of quarrel, and his father never returned to the apartment where Alex lived with his mother.

Immediately after the Revolution, when Alex was just six, his mother got a visa to work in Germany for three years. They lived in an apartment in Berlin while his mother worked as a barmaid. Alex began to attend school and finished grades one through three before he and his mother returned to Romania. When he wasn't in school, Alex's mother insisted he remained locked up in the apartment. He had nothing to do but watch TV; he was very bored. Added to the unhappiness and loneliness was the fact that his mother resented him—that his existence interfered with her life. She became increasingly distant and hostile toward him—even cursed him.

When they returned to Romania, Alex had forgotten the Romanian language and had to pick it up all over again. His mother got a job as a barmaid in Bucharest and put Alex in a kind of boarding school where he came home only on weekends. But eventually, Alex's presence even on weekends was annoying, so she placed him in an orphanage, telling him he would have to stay only a year and then she would come back for him.

Alex did not see his mother the entire year; when she didn't show up to get him, he escaped and went looking for her. Surprisingly (for Bucharest is quite large and confusing) Alex found the apartment and rang the bell. When his mother saw him, she screamed, "You! What are you doing here?"

"I came to find you. I want to stay here with you and not at the orphanage any more."

At that, his mother took off her shoe and hit Alex on the head. "Get out of here," she screamed. "I don't ever want to see you again!"

Alex walked slowly down the stairs and out into the street. He was ten years old. Life in the orphanage had been unpleasant. The food was not enough, and the staff was always beating the children while cursing and screaming at them. He made his decision; he would not go back.

Nearby was the entrance to the Bucharest subway system: the Titan Metro Station. He walked down the stairs into the underground complex. There were kiosks that lined the passageways: small shops that sold newspapers or snacks or gift items. Alex walked around and around, familiarizing himself with the area. Eventually he met a couple of street kids who lived in the station and struck up a kind of friendship with them. They showed him the ropes of living on the streets. Summer and winter, cold and heat, Alex lived in the concrete underground the next two and a half years. Those beginning the life of a street child soon learn how best to survive. In Alex's case, he found he was good at stealing. He also struck up a friendship with the owner of one of the kiosks who gave him odd jobs to do in return for food, cigarettes or a few coins. It was always important that the street kids made their peace—got in good with the police. The police had a lot of dirty work they didn't like to do, or legally couldn't do, and often put the street kids to doing it for them in return for leaving the kids alone. Alex is haunted by the memories to this day.

When Alex was in the orphanage, a group came one summer from Germany to help with the children, and they discovered Alex spoke fluent German. Of course, they took a great interest in him because of that. The next year they were dismayed that Alex was gone—but no one knew where. Alex was twelve and a half years old another year later when the group came once again from Germany. They were passing through the subway station when they spotted him. What are you doing here?" they asked. When Alex told them, they insisted on finding him a proper home. No place in Bucharest would receive him, so they started driving north. Project after project was visited—

but no one wanted the boy. Finally, through a chance word, they heard about our place, 225 miles north of Bucharest.

When they rang the bell and I invited them in, they told me they had a twelve-year-old out in the car, asleep, and hoped they could place him with me. I told them outright that I was full and couldn't take in any more children. I was sorry. They asked if I would at least just meet the boy, so I agreed they could bring him in.

I was impressed at how clean he was in appearance and how polite he was. I felt there was something very special about the boy, and something nudged me to make room for him and give him a chance.

When I told them I would accept Alex, they were incredulous. "You will? You will?" they kept saying over and over. "We have been all over Romania with him."

In the days, weeks and months that followed I had good cause to question my accepting him because I realized I had another sociopath on my hands. And no wonder. He was an unwanted child, openly rejected by his mother, never knowing his father, unbonded, a series of bad experiences in the orphanage and on the streets: a perfect incubator.

When any child comes to our home, the first three days are the honeymoon. We never really know what we have until after the third day. So with Alex. Then the anger began to surface. He had a tongue that could sear paint off the wall, and he shouted invectives at everyone around him. That was only the opening scene. In the next year or so, Alex ran away sixteen times. Three times he stole money when he left—and not small sums. So I had him picked up by the police and put twice in the local juvenile detention center. The second time, his mother heard about it and came to see Alex. I went with her to the detention center, and we sat at a table and talked. During the conversation she reached out her hand and tried to put it on his arm. Alex jumped back as if bitten by a snake. I found it curious to watch.

The third time he stole and ran, he headed for Bucharest, so I called a police friend and had him picked up as he got off the train. That time I determined to leave him rot in the detention center. Finally, after a couple months of it he broke and sent a neighbor, who had gone to visit him, to us with an olive branch. I arranged to have him released, and he returned in February 1998. Alex behaved quite well after that and always referred to his incarceration as, "When I was on vacation."

In early April the thought began to come to me, "You are to adopt Alex." It would seem like a crazy thing to do. Adopt a sociopath?

Three weeks later I sat down by Alex's bedside one evening just to chat. "You know," he began, "I had a lot of time to think while on vacation. I analyzed my situation and what I needed to rise out of it. I came to the conclusion I need a family: a real family—a real mother and a real father." Then he blurted out, "Would you adopt me?"

Because I had already thought about it, I was not surprised by his request. I told him I needed time to think about it and talk to my wife, Deana. We decided. Yes.

The process took fifteen months—way longer than it should have—but the mills of God grind faster than the

Romanian bureaucracy.

The story is not over. First, we have to examine what had happened up to this point. Some kind of miracle it was: An unbonded, antisocial child had become attached. He had found an island of stability in a sea of turmoil. For Alex it meant everything in the world. He now had real parents, a real family, and our children became his brothers and sisters. Because most Americans cannot pronounce my German last name, the name has been somewhat of a trial to me all my life. But to Alex who spoke German and who identified with Germany more than Romania, it was the most beautiful name he had ever heard. He went downtown, found a letter K on a chain and wore it around his neck even before the adoption was finalized. Occasionally one gets lost, but he always replaces it.

I took Alex to America twice where he met the rest of the family—his new brothers and sisters. Now comes the painful part.

Certain tensions often arise within a family as children enter adolescence. Often, where there is a problem, it centers around the child's budding independence. All five of our children hit adolescence at the same time, so the possibilities of conflict were high. Added to this was the fact that I was teaching the high school department of the Christian school where we lived and had my children in class.

One of my children (I'll call him or her T___) never quite resolved the problem and carried it into adulthood, even though we had attempted to talk it out and resolve it.

Alex wanted to get to know each of our children individually, so I arranged to visit the city were T___ lived and for them to spend time together. After Alex and I returned to where we were headquartering during the trip, I noticed he was rather sullen and uncooperative. I paid no attention until the fourth day, when his change of attitude could no longer be ignored.

Alex and I have always communicated very well. Both of us feel free to come on directly, so I commented on his conduct and asked what was the problem. I was appalled to hear, then, that T___ had spent the time with Alex bringing up the past and complaining of me.

In Romania, I was totally respected. Alex had never heard anyone speak against me. The foundation of my project was a phrase I designed, "I respect you; you respect me." My respect for the boys and girls we cared for was very high, and they returned that respect. But now, one of my own children was criticizing me and putting doubts in Alex's mind. His world was shattered. The man he held up as an absolute ideal, who had rescued him from the streets and even made him his own son, was denounced as unworthy of respect. He could not cope with it. His island of stability had sunk into the sea, and he was, once again, adrift. It was a disaster. The one, single thing that could cure a sociopath had been thoughtlessly demolished.

I talked it over with Alex, all that had been said to him, and Alex realized there was no substance to it. And even if there had been any substance, T___ was not showing proper judgment in dragging Alex into a conflict that had happened before he was born. Yet, the bonding stability a sociopath needs cannot be reconstructed overnight. In this case, it took well over a year, and what happened during that year was so horrible I do not care to set it down on paper. I emerged from that year with my health ruined, my serenity shattered, Alex performing once again as a sociopath and myself several thousand dollars poorer.

Now, at last, I feel stability has been restored and that Alex and I are bonded again. Before that happened, there was one more step that had to be taken, and I mention this because it is important if one wants to understand the sociopath.

The sociopath is filled with rage—not anger, but rage. This is the fuel that drives their engine. A young child, mistreated, cannot retaliate against his abuser. The frustration of being unable to defend oneself, of being helpless, is converted into rage, and it accumulates. The rage is eventually transferred onto society, and retaliation becomes an obsession. Everyone, then, becomes the sociopath's enemy and, ultimately, victim. Over and over these sociopathic children have told me, "No one ever loved me in my whole life," and, "I have never had a real friend." The pity is that they start out accepting my offer of friendship and parental love, and a great peace and happiness floods into their souls, but it seems impossible for them to hold that position for very long. In the beginning, kindness appears to mean something to them, but in the long run they view it as a weakness—and I have been told that directly: that my greatest mistake is that I am too kind. I believe that Alex was attracted to me more by my putting him in detention three times than he was by any kindness I showed him.

Toward the end of the renewal period of my relationship

with Alex we hit another wall of conflict just when I thought things were about resolved. He announced he wanted to go to Bucharest for several days, and I said no. For one thing, he was in school, and, for another, he must put Bucharest behind him. We came nose to nose on it. It was one thing I would not yield on. He was as determined to go as I was not to let him. In working with teens, I always attempt to bring them around to thinking they are the ones making the decision that is best for them, whereas, in reality, I have steered them in that direction. But in this case I started using words with Alex like *forbid*. When I did, Alex broke. He told me he wanted to go find his biological father, whom he could not remember. He just wanted to ask him to his face why he abandoned him, why he never had a childhood, never a birthday or Christmas, nor a family nor friend; why he had to sleep in a subway station on cold concrete. "I just have to hear it from him," Alex said. By that time he was crying, and I don't recall ever seeing him cry before.

I said I thought it was a great idea and that I would gladly pay his expenses. So he went. I had no idea what he faced. We had our own problems with the man when we were adopting Alex. We had to have his biological father's signature, and I sent our business manager to get it. At first the man refused, but when our manager insisted, the man said he would sign for $200. That did not sit well with Alex: being sold for $200. As Alex left, I reminded him that the man was no longer his father; that I am.

He arrived home at 1:00 A.M., so I didn't get to talk to him until the next morning when I sat at his bedside. I took one look and realized I was seeing a different person. Something surely amazing had happened.

Alex found his father's apartment and had to wait a long time for him to come home. The man is now sixty years old and a taxi driver, though we understand he had been a person of some importance in the past. When the man saw Alex at his door he asked, "Who are you?"

Alex replied, "I'm Alex, your son."

"What?" the man exploded. "You little bastard! Didn't your mother tell you never to come looking for me?"

"Look, I didn't come to make trouble. I just wanted to know who you are and to talk to you."

The man let out a string of curses. By this time, the ruckus attracted the neighbors in the apartment building who commented, "Why Mr. C___, we didn't know you had another son."

"I told you," broke in Alex, "I don't want any trouble. I don't want any money or anything from you. I just want to talk to you."

At that, the man swung at Alex, who is six feet tall, and hit him in the chest. Alex, in turn, swung back, knocked the man to the floor, spit in his face and walked out.

Since then, Alex has been a different person. The rage is gone. He speaks more softly now and more kindly. He often goes downtown to buy sandwiches for street kids and elderly, homeless women. He also goes to the local orphanage every Saturday to play with the orphans and try to bring them some happiness.

I told Alex that he had not exactly handled the situation with his biological father as the Bible recommends, but that if he had any trouble with the Lord over it, I would stand with him on the Day of Judgment.

I realize not every sociopath can be adopted—nor should they be. But unless they bond to someone, unless they forgive their tormentors from the past, unless they exhaust their rage and, I believe, unless they find peace with God through Jesus, there will be no change and no healing of their condition.

Subsequently, I began to address the issue of guilt and rage with some of the other children in our care. We discussed where to place the blame for their condition; we discussed the fountain of rage and its origin; we discussed facing the past with boldness and not hiding these things anymore; and, most of all, I told them it was all right to cry. And many of them did.

I continue to search for methods, and my heart and admiration go out to anyone who chooses to work with this kind of child.

(As of August 2002, Alex lives in the United States, is an American citizen and works in a nursing home as a certified nursing assistant caring for the elderly.)

MINISTRY INFORMATION

The work about which you have just read is sponsored by the Christian Mission to Youth, Inc., a private, nonprofit organization founded in 1970 by John M. Kachelmyer and recognized by the IRS for tax-deductible contributions.

The mission was founded at the height of the youth revolution of the late 1960s and early 1970s to assist and rehabilitate alienated youth. Later the mission backed seventeen years of work in Honduras.

Since January 1993, the mission's sole purpose is to provide financial support to the Romanian project. It should be noted that since 1999 the intent of the project has changed. It no longer accepts homeless children for rehabilitation since numerous projects have arisen to meet those needs. Rather, the former street children, now rehabilitated, who remain within the project are engaged in humanitarian aid and evangelistic work with the impoverished Gypsy community. Feeding programs for several hundred children and aid of all types are extended to the Gypsies. Romania contains the largest Gypsy population in the word, and the condition of its children, in many ways, is comparable to the misery of the street children.

The mission does not make financial appeals or engage

in fund-raising as such. It depends upon the generosity of those who hear of the project want to be a part of it and choose to support it. Financial support is gratefully received, and a newsletter is sent to supporters.

Those who wish to write or to support the project may contact:

Christian Mission to Youth, Inc. (or CMY, Inc.)
P. O. Box 511
Belen, NM 87002

A Bucharest Street

Just off the street

After clean-up

The famous Gara de Nord

Catalin's parents

Children enjoying
John's sandwiches

Catalin at age 17

Catalin in back left at age 15

Catalin and Alex with Senator
Mary Landrieu in the Senate din-
ing room, Washington, DC, 2001

A street child who has slashed
his own arm with glass.

Catalin with his siblings

Catalin's new home

Catalin at bottom with house-
mates (former street kids)

Costel, center,
while on the streets

John and Costel a few days later

Costel, with Alex,
a few years later

CHILDREN OF THE STREET

"Sniffing" Aurolac

No place to sleep